ETSY

BUSINESS

A Comprehensive Guide on How to Start a Six Figure Etsy Shop

FRAN WILLIAMS

Table of Contents

INTRODUCTION

Have you ever dreamed of starting an online business and being your own boss? Imagine waking up when you want, working on projects you're passionate about, and earning a full-time income from the comfort of your home. Opening an Etsy shop will make this dream a reality.

This comprehensive guide teaches you how to build a profitable Etsy shop from scratch. Whether you have no prior experience selling online or are looking to take your existing shop to the next level, you'll find strategies and insights to help you thrive on Etsy's global marketplace.

The guide begins with essential groundwork, discussing how to identify the right product niche for you, choosing a brand name and style, and finding reliable suppliers and manufacturers to produce your products. You'll learn the pros and cons of manufacturing your inventory versus using print-on-demand services to drop ship orders to customers. Also, the book provides a checklist of key tasks to complete before opening your Etsy shop.

Next, the book discusses the details of setting up your Etsy shop for success. You will learn how to craft compelling listing titles, tags, descriptions, and photos to attract buyers. You'll discover pricing and shipping strategies to maximize profits and keep customers happy. You'll find the best tips for making your shop stand out with a polished brand, great customer service, and smart SEO tactics.

Once your shop is up and running, it's time to start generating sales. The book goes on to explain effective promotional approaches on Etsy and beyond, like running ads, cultivating organic social media buzz, and optimizing your shop for search engine visibility. You'll learn strategies for incentivizing those crucial first sales and reviews from family, friends, and early customers.

Managing the day-to-day operations of an Etsy shop is key for long-term growth. You'll find the best practices for providing five-star customer service, handling issues like copyright claims and negative reviews, and streamlining order fulfillment. The book also shares time management and productivity hacks for running your business smoothly.

To take your success to the next level, this book includes advanced Etsy selling strategies like analyzing competitor shops, finding underserved niche markets, creating unique products, and experimenting with discounts and sales. You'll discover tools and resources for gaining valuable insights into customer demand, upcoming trends, and opportunities for innovation.

By the end, you'll have the confidence and expertise to transform your hobby into a thriving Etsy shop. Whether you're looking to earn supplemental income or eventually quit your day job, you'll find all the insider tips you need to make your entrepreneurial dreams a reality.

CHAPTER 1

THINGS TO DO BEFORE OPENING AN ETSY SHOP

Before you open up shop, there are a few key steps you need to take to set yourself up for success. In this chapter, you'll learn the basics of Etsy's business model to help you create an informed business plan. Next, you'll learn the process of choosing a niche and products based on your skills, interests, and target audience.

The chapter explains the pros and cons of selling under your brand name versus generic products. It'll briefly discuss finding suppliers and manufacturers. Finally, you will get a checklist summarizing the essential tasks to complete before opening your online doors. With the groundwork laid out, you'll be armed with the knowledge to start your Etsy shop.

Understanding Etsy's Business Model

Etsy is a popular e-commerce marketplace for artists, craftspeople, vintage sellers, and other creative entrepreneurs to turn their hobbies and skills into successful businesses. Etsy focuses on handmade, vintage, and craft products, unlike mass retailers like Amazon or eBay.

As an aspiring Etsy seller, you should understand the inner workings of the marketplace's business model before opening your shop. That will help you make informed decisions about your shop setup, product offerings, pricing strategies, and target audience.

Etsy's History and Mission

To understand Etsy's unique business model, it helps to first look at its history. Etsy was founded in 2005 in Brooklyn, New York, by Robert Kalin, Chris Maguire, Haim Schoppik, and Jared Tarbell.

The founders aimed to create an online marketplace focusing on showcasing independent artists, craftspeople, vintage sellers, and other creative small business owners. Their mission was to provide an alternative to mass-manufactured products by connecting artisan sellers with buyers seeking quality, handmade goods.

According to an article by JungleWorks, the name Etsy comes from a mix of "etymology", which is the study of words' origins, and "economy". This highlights the company's goal of building a new economic model around small-scale creators instead of major corporations.

Etsy emphasizes the values of inspiration, inclusivity, imagination, and innovation. The company describes its purpose as keeping commerce human by nurturing a community-focused marketplace. This creator-driven ethos informs Etsy's business strategies.

How Does Etsy Make Money?

As an e-commerce marketplace, Etsy earns revenue through five primary streams:

1. Seller Transaction Fees

Etsy charges various fees for sellers to list products and complete sales. These include listing fees per item, transaction fees per sale, and payment processing fees. Transaction fees are Etsy's main revenue source.

2. Etsy Ads Program

Etsy allows sellers to pay for sponsored product listings and banner ads to increase visibility. Fees from these ads are a growing source of revenue.

3. Subscription and Services Revenue

Etsy earns money through charging monthly subscriptions for premium seller features. The company also provides paid coaching and consulting services.

4. Shipping Labels

By selling shipping labels to sellers and taking a percentage of the label price, Etsy brings in substantial revenue.

5. Gift Cards

The company sells gift cards to buyers and gains income from unredeemed gift card balances.

While advertising and subscription services are increasing revenue streams, Etsy still largely relies on charging listing and transaction fees to make money. Understanding Etsy's standard fees is key for assessing potential costs as a seller.

Etsy's Seller Fees

Etsy levies a range of different fees on shop owners to list, sell, and manage their shops. It's crucial to factor in these fees when pricing items and calculating potential profit margins. The main fees include:

- **Listing Fees -** $0.20 per item listed, with listings expiring after 4 months. You can renew for an additional $0.20. No limit on the number of listings.

- **Transaction Fees -** 5% of the item price + shipping. E.g., $50 item + $5 shipping = $55. 5% of $55 is a $2.75 transaction fee.

- **Payment Processing Fees -** For Etsy Payments, it's 3% of order total + $0.25 per order. Offsite payments like PayPal incur 3.5% of the order total.

- **Ads Fee -** 12% of the order total if the order came from an ad click.

- **Pattern Fee -** 15% fee on high-volume digital orders after surpassing 100 digital orders.

- **Shipping Label Fees -** Etsy charges more than USPS retail rates for labels, pocketing the difference.

- **Gift Wrapping Charges -** Etsy takes a 25% cut of gift wrapping surcharges.

- **Monthly Subscription -** $10-$40/month subscription for premium shop features.

These are Etsy's standard fees. However, the company provides ways to potentially lower fees. You'll learn more about that later on.

When starting, listing fees of $0.20 per item and low transaction fees make Etsy an appealing option. But at higher volumes, the numerous recurring fees can quickly eat into profits. Understanding the fee structure helps you plan pricing and margins.

Payment Processing on Etsy

Payment processing costs constitute a major business expense for Etsy sellers. Etsy Payments is the company's integrated payment processing system. It charges domestic sellers 3% of the order total plus $0.25 per transaction.

By comparison, offsite payments via PayPal incur a higher 3.5% of order total fee since Etsy has to share revenue.

Both Etsy Payments and PayPal deposit funds directly into your bank account. Etsy Payments is the simpler option for new sellers since it's built-in. But the recurring 3% + $0.25 per order can add up quickly. Alternatives like Stripe and Square offer competitive rates starting around 2.6% to 2.9% per transaction.

Overall, high-volume sellers would do well to explore lower-cost external processors. For those just starting out, Etsy Payments is the best choice. As your shop scales, re-assess to potentially reduce fees.

The Etsy Ads Program

Etsy's advertising platform is a major component of its business model. Etsy Ads allow shop owners to pay for Sponsored Listings that appear prominently in search results above regular listings. Like most ad programs, you can set a daily budget. Bids start at around $0.10 per click.

Over 60% of Etsy sellers now use Sponsored Listings, which can increase product visibility. However, there are some potential disadvantages:

- Costs add up quickly, which cuts into profit margins.

- Etsy charges an extra 12% fee on sales from ads.

- Shops with higher ad budgets tend to dominate. This makes it tough for new sellers to compete.

- There is a risk of overspending the daily budget.

For new Etsy shops, focusing on SEO and product listings initially is a smarter move than paid. Once you have consistent organic traffic, ads can supplement but shouldn't replace organic strategies.

Pros of Etsy's Model

- Low barriers to entry for sellers. Just $0.20 per listing.

- Built-in marketplace with over 60 million potential buyers.

- No need to build your website. Etsy handles everything.

- Can leverage existing skills and inventory you have on hand.

- Strong brand recognition. Buyers trust Etsy for unique handmade goods.

Cons of Etsy's Model

- Highly competitive marketplace. Over 4 million active shops.

- Recurring fees like transaction fees reduce profit over time.

- Little control over customizing your shop's branding and layout.

- Frequent policy changes can disrupt seller operations.

Etsy offers an easy entry point thanks to low upfront costs and instant access to buyers. However, limitations around branding, fees, and policy changes are worth considering for established sellers.

There's no definitive right or wrong answer. Consider if the pros outweigh the cons. Etsy is a great launching pad while selling across multiple channels, or your site is better for scaling.

Comparing Etsy to Handmade Marketplace Alternatives

To decide if Etsy is the best option, it's useful to compare Etsy to other craft-focused marketplaces. Each has pros and cons.

ArtFire

- Lower 5% transaction fees.

- Allows manufacturers and wholesalers.

- Much lower site traffic than on Etsy.

Dawanda

- Based in Germany.

- Primarily European sellers and buyers.

- 5% transaction fees.

Amazon Handmade

- Must have an Amazon seller account.

- 12-15% referral fees per item sold.

Zibbet

- 8.5% transaction fees.

- Smaller market but tight-knit community.

- Useful coaching resources.

Shopify

- $29+ monthly subscription fee.

- Complete control over branding and sales channels.

- Higher startup costs and technical skills needed.

SquareSpace

- $12+ monthly subscription fee.

- Website builder and hosting.

- Not as handmade-focused as Etsy.

Goimagine

- Made for UK sellers.

- £0.20 listing fee plus 3.5% transaction fee.

- Much lower traffic than Etsy.

Folksy

- Made in the UK for UK sellers/buyers.

- £0.20 listing fee plus 3.5% transaction fee.

- Significantly lower site traffic than Etsy.

Competitor platforms may offer lower fees in some cases and greater customization than your shop. However, Etsy still dominates the handmade marketplace space in terms of total active buyers and sellers. Etsy's brand recognition and site traffic gives new sellers a major leg up.

More established sellers may eventually transition to their independent website or diversify across multiple platforms for greater control over branding, fees, features, and audience reach. But Etsy provides an easy starting point for validating and launching a handmade business concept quickly.

Key Questions to Consider

Given this comprehensive look at Etsy's business model components and alternatives, here are some key questions to ask yourself when deciding if Etsy is the right sales channel:

- Are you just testing an idea before investing in a standalone site?

- Is Etsy's built-in marketplace exposure and large buyer base important for your launch?

- Can you accept Etsy's more rigid shop customization and policies in exchange for access to more buyers?

- Are Etsy's numerous fees and substantial competition prohibitive for your profit goals?

- Is your business at a stage where investing in your independent website makes more strategic sense?

- Can you differentiate yourself enough on Etsy, or should you also explore other handmade marketplaces?

- What unique opportunities on Etsy can you take advantage of?

Your answers will depend on your business model, priorities, stage of growth, and available resources.

Many sellers successfully start on Etsy to test and validate their concept without major upfront investment. To maximize branding freedom and profitability long-term, however, diversifying your site or additional sales channels may become beneficial.

Deciding What to Sell

One of the most important decisions when starting an Etsy shop is determining the product to sell. With over 60 million active buyers visiting Etsy for unique, handmade, and vintage items, the possibilities are virtually endless.

It's tempting to try selling a little bit of everything in your new Etsy store. But taking a strategic, focused approach to choosing your products gives you the best chance of standing out in this competitive marketplace.

The following are some tactics you can use to find your niche, evaluate product ideas, understand customer demand, and set your shop up for success.

Conduct a Self-Assessment

Begin your product selection process by doing an honest self-assessment. Reflect on the following questions:

- What crafting skills, hobbies, or artistic talents can you leverage for product ideas?

- What raw materials, tools, and equipment do you have on hand to get started?

- How much space and initial startup budget do you have?

- How much time can you commit each week to production and shop management?

- At what pricing range are you comfortable selling your products?

Knowing your existing assets and limitations helps narrow down viable product options. For example, if you're great at woodworking and painting, you could make custom home decor signs. If sewing is your specialty, consider handmade tote bags or baby clothes.

Think through what you're naturally good at or most passionate about, as creativity and enthusiasm will come through in your products. Also, consider any background in photography, graphic design, or branding that could help you create professional listings.

Take stock of your available workspace, startup budget, and the hourly time you can dedicate before and after your regular job if you initially plan to run your Etsy shop as a side business. This will help frame realistic production capabilities and inventory levels you can handle.

Pick Your Top Product Categories

Once you've reflected on your skills and resources, make a shortlist of three to five broad product categories that interest you and align with what you could feasibly make and sell.

If you're an avid knitter, knitted accessories would be an obvious choice. If you want to sell vintage items, vintage clothing or retro home goods are potential categories.

Think through not just what you can make yourself but what types of products inspire you and will bring satisfaction as part of your daily workflow.

Here are some of the most popular product categories to consider:

- Jewelry

- Clothing and accessories

- Home décor

- Paper and party supplies

- Bath and beauty products

- Toys and games

- Pet products

- Kitchen and dining goods

- Wedding supplies

- Woodworking

- Upcycled and eco-friendly products

Once you've narrowed down the list of categories, you'll move to a specific item selection.

Dive Deep into Potential Products

The next step is researching specific products within your categories of interest to assess their viability. Here are some key factors to evaluate:

a. Target Customer

Who is your target audience? Young adults, families with kids, pet owners? Defining your ideal customer helps guide product decisions.

For example, if stay-at-home moms are your target, baby blankets or nursery wall signs may be a fit. If teens and young adults are your audience, funky jewelry and dorm decor are routes to explore.

b. Competition

Browse Etsy to gauge existing competition for a potential product. Use specific keyword phrases like "handmade copper bracelets" or "vintage flower shirts." If you see pages and pages of results, competition will be high. Try finding less saturated niche opportunities.

c. Production Costs

Factor in the hands-on time, labor, and material costs involved in producing a prospective item. Estimate how long it will take you to make each product and the cost of raw materials. This informs the minimum price you'll need to charge to turn a profit.

d. Pricing

On a similar note, research Etsy to understand the typical pricing range for your product idea. Look up listings for similar items to see the prices they charge. Your pricing should align with customer expectations while covering production costs.

e. Profit Margin

After subtracting costs, calculate the potential profit margin per item. Account for Etsy's listing, transaction, and processing fees, too. Aim for at least a 50-100% profit margin per piece.

f. Uniqueness

Does your product idea offer something special compared to competitors? Unique color palettes, materials, or designs help your products stand out and allow you to set higher prices.

g. Trends

Look at Etsy's trending searches and product categories to align with rising demand. You should also consider whether the trend has sustainable longevity.

Evaluating these factors will reveal which product ideas have the most potential for your Etsy shop. You want options with reasonable startup costs that fill a customer's need with room for profit even after Etsy fees.

Find Your Niche

Within your broader product categories, finding a tightly defined niche is key to Etsy's success. This could mean targeting very specific:

- **Customer Demographics** - like geeky college students or minimalist moms

- **Hobbies and Interests** - like yoga, gardening, or astrology

- **Product Attributes** - like copper jewelry, succulent planters, or neutral nursery decor

- **Geographic Regions** - like Southern U.S. lifestyle products or London-themed gifts

- **Occasions** - like bridal shower party favors or anniversary presents

A niche focuses your products, brand image, listings, and shop layout around highly targeted themes and customer segments. This helps you excel at meeting the needs of a specific group instead of getting lost in the sea of generic shops.

Validate Demand

Once you've narrowed down product possibilities through self-assessment and research, it's time to validate actual demand. Here are two quick tips:

- Run a poll on social media asking friends, family, or existing followers to vote on their favorite product ideas. See which concepts generate excitement.

15

- List test products on Etsy and spend $20-$50 promoting them with Etsy Ads. If you get ad clicks and favorites, demand looks promising.

Validating with real potential customers gives you confidence in an idea before investing in full production and inventory.

Align with Your Brand

Make sure your products fit the brand image you want for your Etsy shop. The products you sell will shape customers' perceptions of your business.

For example, selling nature-inspired wood signs fits well with an earthy, bohemian brand identity. Selling feminist slogan shirts complements a bold, progressive brand persona.

Think through the experience you want customers to have when browsing your shop and how your products can consistently reinforce this.

Adapt and Test New Products

One advantage of Etsy is you can easily test adding new products once your shop is up and running. Pay attention to customer feedback.

Favorable reviews and sales for a new item signal positive response. If customers don't seem intrigued, or you have to deeply discount a product to move units, consider removing it from your lineup.

Etsy's platform makes it easy to experiment with new products over time as you identify opportunities.

Do Your Research

Conducting thorough research is crucial to identify and validate the right products. Here are some tips:

1. **Search Etsy Bestsellers** - Look at current bestselling items in your product categories. Sort search results by "Best Match" then "All Time." See what consistently sells.

2. **Monitor Emerging Trends** - Use Etsy's Trending Searches page to see rising product ideas. But also watch for oversaturated trends on their way out.

3. **Study Competitors** - Order samples from Etsy competitors selling similar products. Analyze pricing, product quality, reviews, and shop branding.

4. **Learn from Local Shops** - Visit craft fairs and small boutiques near you. Observe what they sell and what customers purchase.

5. **Use E-Commerce Tools** - Try e-commerce product research tools like Etsy Rank and Marmalead to analyze competing listings and popular keywords.

6. **Read Forums** - Check Etsy and e-commerce forums for insider advice on opportunities and saturated markets. Listen to experienced sellers.

7. **Validate with Polls** - Run simple polls on social media or survey tools to get feedback on product concepts from potential buyers.

Casting a wide research net helps you gain 360-degree visibility into customer preferences, gaps in the market, and products poised for success.

Think Long-Term

It's tempting to only consider current bestsellers and trends when picking products. But you should also think about long-term sustainability.

- These are some questions you need to ask yourself when evaluating longevity:

- Does this product have lasting appeal, or is it just a fleeting trend?

- Are the required materials and components available long-term?

- Can you envision making this product without getting bored for the next 1-2 years?

- Does it fit with my brand identity in the long run?

- Is there room to build a family of products around this initial idea?

You don't want to risk investing a lot of time and resources into a product idea that will eventually burn out. Look for items that can be part of your product mix for years to come.

For example, simple jewelry designs, classic baby items like quilts, or personalized home décor signs tend to stand the test of time.

Start Small

When first opening your Etsy shop, it's wise to start small and targeted with just one or two product types instead of offering a huge assortment out the gate.

Some advantages to a narrow initial product focus include:

- Giving you the chance to perfect your production process and quality for those items.

- Reducing materials costs in the startup phase.

- Creating cohesive branding and shop layout easily.

- Helping you understand customer response to refine the product.

- Having fewer items to juggle as a first-time seller.

You can always expand your product catalog down the road. Limiting yourself to one or two best-selling products to start reduces risk and complexity.

Tell a Story

Regardless of your chosen product, think about how you can tell an engaging backstory about the items in your Etsy listings.

- Share details like:

- The creative process behind designing the product.

- How you hand-select the special materials used.

- Your journey learning production skills.

- What inspired you to start selling this particular item?

These types of stories help buyers connect with you. Stories also boost SEO and sales conversion rates, which is a win-win.

At every step of evaluating potential products, keep your skills, brand, ideal customer, competitors, costs, and long-term goals at the front of your mind. With rigorous analysis and validation, you'll easily choose to win Etsy products positioned for sustainable success.

Common Etsy Products to Consider

While conducting your custom research is essential, it helps to consider proven top-selling products on Etsy as a starting point for inspiration.

Here are some of the most popular Etsy products and categories:

Jewelry

- Jewelry consistently dominates Etsy's top sales. Common winning products include necklaces, rings, earrings, and bracelets. Focus on unique materials like gemstones, wood, enamel, or engraved metals. Niche down into specific styles like boho chic, minimalist, or personalized jewelry.

Clothing

- Apparel is another great seller. Consider starting with accessories like scarves, hats, and headbands, which require less materials and labor than clothes. Then, expand into clothing like dresses, tops, or baby onesies. Vintage and upcycled clothing also sell well.

Home Decor

- Wall art, pillows, mirrors, and organizational items like storage bins and baskets are hot sellers. Infuse your style into decor with colors, prints, textures, or clever sayings. Zero in on a specific room like the nursery, kitchen, or bathroom.

Paper Goods

- Etsy buyers love stationery, wall prints, calendars, greeting cards, and party supplies like banners and confetti. Include personalized details to make items feel extra special. Aim for beautiful photography and typography.

Gifts

- Help customers check off their gift list with presents like candles, beauty products, pet supplies, children's toys, and gourmet food items. Build gift sets around occasions like birthdays, Christmas, Mother's Day, anniversaries, and weddings.

Craft Supplies

- Other Etsy sellers need supplies for their shops. Cater to fellow makers with specialty items like washi tape, sewing patterns, stamp sets, and crochet kits. You can even teach hard skills through how-to guides.

There are proven options to help spark product ideas suited for Etsy. Bring your creative twist and backstory to any product you pursue to stand out.

Are You Ready to Open Your Etsy Shop?

Deciding on the right products to sell is one of the most critical steps to creating a successful business. Take your time researching ideas, analyzing competitors, validating demand, exploring niches, and finding the perfect fit.

By putting in enough thought and effort upfront, you'll have the confidence that your products are positioned for sustainable results.

Branded or Generic?

One strategic decision to make when setting up your Etsy shop is whether to sell products under a unique brand name or opt for a generic, unbranded approach.

There are pros and cons to each route. It'll help to know the factors to consider when deciding between building your distinctive brand versus selling unlabeled items on Etsy.

Benefits of Creating Your Brand

While listing products without any specific brand name is certainly an option on Etsy, intentionally developing your own brand identity offers some major advantages:

1. **Memorability**

   A strong brand gives customers something memorable to latch onto. A creative brand name, logo, and packaging design are more likely to stick in customers' minds and be associated with positive shopping experiences.

2. **Trust**

   Consistent branding creates familiarity and trust with buyers over time. They begin to recognize and rely on interacting with your brand specifically vs. generic unbranded sellers.

3. **Loyalty**

   Customers who identify with your brand values and style are much more likely to become repeat loyal buyers who regularly shop at your store vs. one-time purchasers.

4. **Higher Prices**

Branded products can often command higher prices than generic unlabeled goods. Customers see added value in the brand identity and are willing to pay more for it.

5. **Enjoyment**

Coming up with fun branding is hugely rewarding and fulfilling for you as a maker. You get to bring your creative vision to life.

6. **Standing Out**

A brand differentiates you from the 4+ million other sellers on Etsy. Without a defined brand, it's much easier to get lost in the shuffle.

Growing a Business

If you ever want to expand beyond Etsy, strong branding establishes the foundation to do so. Your brand identity remains consistent across multiple sales channels.

Building an identifiable brand around your products requires more upfront effort but pays off exponentially.

Your Etsy brand identity will be conveyed through elements like:

- **Brand Name** - A memorable, catchy name that reflects your products or values. Keep in mind that shorter is better.

- **Logo** - A visual emblem uniquely tied to your business. It should be recognizable in small sizes.

- **Color Palette** - 3-5 core colors that customers associate with your brand.

- **Fonts** - 1-2 complementary fonts for listings, packaging, social media, etc.

- **Tone of Voice** - The style and language used consistently across channels.

- **Packaging** - Cohesive labeling and packaging reinforcing the brand.

- **Photography Style** - Consistent image editing, props, and backdrops.

Every visual and written customer touchpoint should reinforce your core identity. Cohesion is key.

When brainstorming brand elements, draw inspiration from the meaning or backstory behind your product line, your target customers, and your personality, values, and quirks. Also, use compelling visual metaphors.

Ultimately, your brand identity should be original and uniquely yours.

Logo Design Tips

As a core brand asset, putting thought into your logo design is key. These are some tips to keep in mind:

Choose a Style

- Minimal, letter-based logos are timeless and flexible. Illustrated logos are friendlier. Research trends and competitors. Most importantly, choose a style that fits your brand personality.

Limit to 2-3 Colors

- Restrict your logo to two or three colors from your core brand palette. Too many colors look unprofessional and are hard to print.

Test Different Fonts

- Experiment with a few font pairings for your logo text. Mixing a simple sans-serif with a more stylistic complementary font works well.

Try Some Graphic Elements

- Consider incorporating visual metaphors like flowers, landscapes, or shapes relevant to your product. Keep it simple with clean lines.

Make It Scalable

- Your logo will need to look right in small sizes, like social media avatars all the way to up to large banner ads. Test scaling it down to make sure it stays recognizable.

Do It Yourself or Hire a Pro

- DIY options like Canva work for simple logos, but hiring a professional graphic designer is worth the investment.

Double Check Licensing

- Make sure any images or fonts you use are commercially licensed for businesses. Steer clear of trademarked clip art or Google Images results.

With strategic planning and design, your Etsy logo will become a beloved brand symbol.

Branding Your Shop Front

With your core branding elements defined, it's time to implement them across your Etsy shop. These elements include:

1. **Banner Image**

   Upload a custom banner incorporating your logo, colors, and imagery. Use bright, high-quality photography representing your products.

2. **Shop Icon**

   Choose a square thumbnail version of your logo as your Etsy shop icon, like your social media profile picture. Keep it crisp and simple.

3. **Shop Name**

   Your Etsy shop's name should align with your brand name for consistency. Choose Etsy username variants if the name you had in mind is taken.

4. **About Section**

   Flesh out your brand story and values in your Etsy About page. Share your inspiration and commitment to quality.

5. **Shop Sections**

Use your color palette and branding in custom sections like "Gift Guide" or "Best Sellers" to reinforce your style.

6. **Packaging**

Order custom packaging materials like stickers, labels, and thank you cards that feature your logo and designs.

7. **Photos**

Maintain a consistent editing style, props, and backdrop for product photos aligned with your branding.

8. **Social Media**

Link your Etsy shop to branded social media business profiles, driving traffic back to your storefront.

Consistent brand presentation boosts professionalism and helps you stand out.

Benefits of Selling Unbranded

While most Etsy sellers focus on establishing their distinctive brand, there are certain advantages to selling quality but unlabeled generic products:

1. **Lower Startup Costs**

You avoid costs associated with professional branding like logo design, packaging, branded social media, etc.

2. **Reduced Effort**

Generic items require less upfront effort to conceptualize branding and implement it across touchpoints.

3. **Flexibility**

You have full flexibility to pivot your product selection without worrying about brand consistency.

4. **Wider Audience**

Some buyers specifically look for generic, non-branded goods on Etsy for lower costs. Casting a wider net brings in more potential customers.

5. **Volume Sales**

Buyers needing multiples of an item for a wedding or event often prefer lower prices over branded goods.

For sellers looking to test the Etsy waters before fully investing in branding, starting with quality but unlabeled products is a smart intro strategy. You can always brand later.

Just make sure your product photos, titles, descriptions, and packaging still look clean and professional - branding or not. Presentation is still key.

Finding a Supplier

Finding the right supplier is a key step in setting up a successful Etsy shop. A good supplier provides quality materials and inventory at affordable prices with reliable order fulfillment.

Keep reading to explore different supplier and manufacturer options for Etsy sellers and tips for evaluating potential suppliers to partner with.

Print-on-Demand Companies

Print-on-demand (POD) companies allow you to design products while they handle printing and order fulfillment. When a customer places an order, the POD service prints and ships the item for you. This saves upfront costs of stocking inventory.

Some popular POD companies used by Etsy sellers include:

- **Printful** - Offers dropshipping for clothing, home goods, and accessories. Integrates with Etsy.

- **Printify** - Provides printing and shipping for various products like mugs, shirts, hats, necklaces, and blankets.

- **Gooten** - Specializes in home décor like wall art, pillows, and tapestries. Good for custom pieces.

- **Teelaunch** - Focuses on t-shirts but offers other products like phone cases, posters, and mugs.

- **Redbubble** - Art-focused POD for apparel, wall art, masks, phone cases, and stickers.

POD is great for new sellers or smaller runs of customizable or seasonal products. Remember to account for their per-item base fees when pricing.

Domestic Manufacturers

For higher volumes, partnering directly with a domestic manufacturer is more affordable. Check sites like Alibaba and Thomasnet to find local-based makers of specific products like furniture, apparel, ceramics, toys, etc.

Vet them thoroughly by requesting references, getting samples, checking reviews, and asking questions about capacity, quality control, and order minimums. You want to ensure reliability when scaling up.

Independent Artisans

Sometimes, the perfect products are made right in your local community by independent artists and craftspeople. Attend craft fairs and markets to network and find talent.

Building personal relationships allows you to ensure quality control and ethical working conditions when sourcing one-of-a-kind handmade goods.

Evaluating Suppliers

Here are key criteria to assess when selecting suppliers:

- **Quality** - Order samples to inspect materials, construction, and durability.

- **Pricing** - Compare per-unit rates across multiple suppliers. Calculate landing costs.

- **Minimums** - Check if minimum order quantities fit your budget and storage capacity.

- **Reliability** - Look for longstanding vendors with positive reviews and quick issue resolution.

- **Capacity** - Do they have the bandwidth to handle your projected order volumes without major delays?

- **Location** - Domestic suppliers provide faster shipping and easier communication.

- **Certifications** - Seek ethical companies with certifications like Fair Trade and OEKO-TEX.

- **Payment Terms** - Aim for Net 30 payment terms after receiving orders. Avoid upfront deposits.

Vetting suppliers thoroughly reduces headaches later on if inventory falls short of your quality standards or shipments get delayed. Taking the time to find reliable partners is always smart.

Managing Multiple Suppliers

Instead of sourcing everything from one vendor, working with several specialized suppliers lets you access unique materials and skills.

For example, you might use one local artisan for ceramic mugs, a Printify for custom t-shirts, and a print vendor for calendars.

Using a supplier management system helps you keep track of contacts, minimums, pricing, and other details so you can easily place reorders across multiple partners.

Checklist

Before you open an Etsy shop, there are several important things you need to do to set your shop up for success.

- First, choose your shop's name carefully. The name is part of your brand, so pick something memorable and descriptive of what you sell. Research keywords to see what terms potential customers look for. Incorporate relevant keywords into your shop name so your listings have a better chance of being found.

- Next, write your Etsy shop announcement. This short blurb is one of the first things potential customers see when they land on your shop's home page. Keep it concise and compelling. Highlight your unique offerings and what makes your shop special. This space is prime real estate for announcing sales or limited edition items too.

- Fill out your Etsy About page thoroughly. This page tells your brand's story. Share how you got started, what inspires you, and why customers should buy from you. Include high-quality photos which give a behind-the-scenes look at your creative process. Make sure to link to your social media accounts so customers can connect with you on multiple platforms.

- Craft your return and exchange policies carefully. Set policies that protect you as a seller but also give customers peace of mind. Use Etsy's policies template, then customize it to fit your specific needs. Be as accommodating as possible. Rigid policies can and will deter buyers. Offer at least a short window for cancellations, refunds, and exchanges.

- Research keywords and SEO best practices. Choose targeted keywords and work them naturally into your listing titles, tags, and descriptions. Place priority keywords at the beginning of titles. Use your full title character allowance. Make sure to expand your reach by using related keywords and phrases too.

- Take high-quality photos that spotlight your products. Crisp, well-lit shots allow shoppers to see exactly what you're selling. Fill all your listing's image slots, centering products against clean backgrounds. Additional shots can showcase extra details, colors, or product uses.

- Set competitive prices, but don't undervalue your work. Research comparable items to find a fair price range. Factor in all your material and labor costs. Price high enough to turn a profit, but not so high that shoppers look elsewhere. You can always lower prices later or run promotional sales.

- Streamline shipping logistics before launch day. Set your shipping policies and charges accurately in your listings. Print shipping labels through Etsy or another service. Prepare packaging materials like boxes, bubble wrap, and tape. Establish packing and shipping processes to save time when orders roll in.

- Connect your Etsy shop to outside marketing channels. Enable Etsy direct checkout on Instagram to get more social media sales. Add links to your online portfolio and email list. Share your shop's custom web address to help customers who want to shop directly. Promote listings on complementary sites like Houzz or Craftsy.

- Plan for holidays and seasonal sales by checking Etsy's key holiday calendar so you can create themed products in advance. Design complementary digital promo graphics to announce specials across social channels and your website. Offer festive discounts or limited edition releases to capitalize on gift-giving spending.

With this checklist, you'll set your Etsy shop up for success from the start. Implement these essential tasks before officially launching to hit the ground running. Following these tips will help you attract customers, drive more sales, and earn glowing reviews right out of the gate.

CHAPTER 2

FINDING A PRODUCTION TEAM OR SUPPLIER

Having a reliable production team or suppliers in place is the foundation for creating quality products at scale. This chapter will explore ways to find partners to handle manufacturing and order fulfillment for your Etsy shop. First, it will look at print-on-demand platforms like Printful and Printify that allow you to easily outsource the production of apparel and home goods.

Next, it will discuss services like ShineOn that specialize in jewelry and provide fulfillment for customizable designs. You will get tips for vetting suppliers based on pricing, quality, capacity, and lead times. By the end of this chapter, you'll have actionable strategies for building a production dream team tailored to your specific product mix. Outsourcing manufacturing and fulfillment allows you to focus on your creative strengths and customer experience.

Printful – Apparel, Mugs, Blankets, etc. (Print on Demand)

One of the most popular production and fulfillment solutions for Etsy sellers is Printful. This print-on-demand (POD) company allows you to focus on designing and selling various products online while it handles manufacturing and shipping your orders.

Printful Overview

Printful is a print-on-demand dropshipping service that integrates with various e-commerce platforms, including Etsy, Shopify, and WooCommerce.

It was founded in 2013 in Latvia. At least 500,000 sellers use Printful globally. It offers on-demand printing, warehousing, and shipping for orders.

Printful integrates directly with Etsy to auto-fulfill orders. It provides a designer tool to mockup product images. It has warehouses in the US, Mexico, and Europe.

The main value proposition of Printful for Etsy sellers is that it enables you to design and sell a wide array of products without handling manufacturing or shipping yourself.

When a customer purchases a product from your Etsy shop, Printful will print it on-demand and ship it out for you. This saves you from dealing with upfront inventory and logistics.

How Printful Works

Here is an overview of how the Printful order fulfillment process works:

1. **Set up Your Etsy Shop**

   First, you'll need an active Etsy shop with listings created. Make sure your shop policies, payment methods, and shipping profiles are configured.

2. **Connect Your Etsy and Printful Accounts**

   In your Printful dashboard, connect your Etsy shop. This allows orders to get automatically imported into Printful.

3. **Create Product Listings**

Using the Printful Mockup Generator, design mockups of your products. Upload to Etsy as listings with Printful SKUs attached.

4. **Customer Places Order**

When a customer purchases your product, the order info is sent to Printful.

5. **Printful Manufactures and Ships Order**

Printful will print the product, pack it, and ship it with your custom branding. You will get an alert when the order is complete.

6. **You Get Paid by Etsy**

After Printful fulfills the order, you receive your payout deposited into your connected Etsy payment account.

Printful handles production and shipping end-to-end, so you can focus entirely on design and sales.

Printful Product Catalog

Printful offers a huge range of products you can customize and sell using their print-on-demand services. Their products include:

- **Apparel:** T-shirts, hoodies, hats, leggings, shorts, and kids' clothes are printed with your custom designs.

- **Bags:** Backpacks, totes, drawstring bags, fanny packs, and duffel bags.

- Home Decor: Tapestries, throw pillows, blankets, shower curtains, and wall art.

- **Phone Cases:** Printful offers phone cases for iPhones, Samsung, and Google Pixel.

- **Jewelry:** Printful can manufacture custom necklaces, bracelets, keychains, and rings.

- **Accessories:** Face masks, bandanas, scarves, socks, pins, and mugs.

They provide tons of product customization options like colors, sizes, and variations.

Printful does not currently offer some products like shoes, beauty items, or food/perishables.

Printful Integrations

A major benefit of Printful for Etsy sellers is its seamless integrations that automatically sync with your stores.

When you connect your Etsy shop to your Printful account settings, every order placed on Etsy will automatically be imported into your Printful dashboard for fulfillment.

This removes the manual work of transferring orders between platforms. It also pushes tracking info and order status back into your Etsy account.

The direct Printful integration makes the entire order fulfillment process smooth and hands-off for Etsy store owners.

Printful has guides to help you connect your Etsy store in a few quick steps. Just make sure that your Etsy shop policies are properly configured first.

Printful Pricing and Fees

When weighing Printful as a production partner, you need to account for their product pricing and fee structure.

There are two main costs to factor in:

Base Product Costs

Every Printful product has a base cost per item. This covers the materials and labor. For example, a basic t-shirt starts at $9.80 base cost.

Fulfillment Fees

- Each order incurs Printful fulfillment fees:

- $2.90 flat fulfillment fee per domestic order

- Additional per-item fulfillment fees ($0.30-$3.50)

- 7.5% shipping cost markup

These fees cover warehousing, printing, handling, and bundled US shipping. International shipments incur additional fees.

You'll want to price your Etsy products accordingly to cover Printful costs and leave room for profit. Failure to properly account for their fees is a common pitfall that eats into profit margins.

Printful Order Processing

Understanding the order processing timeline is important when using Printful to manage customer expectations.

After an order is placed on your Etsy shop, here is the typical Printful order fulfillment schedule:

- **Same or next business day** - Order received by Printful.

- **1 business day** - Printful prints and packs order.

- **1 to 5 business days** - In-transit shipping time

- **5 to 8 business days** - Estimated delivery for domestic US orders

- **10 to 15 business days** - Estimated delivery for international orders

Note that production and transit days can vary based on order volume, holidays, etc. Printful provides live support if any issues come up.

You can also offer expedited shipping, like 2-day or next day, to shorten the delivery timeline for customers who want faster turnaround.

Printful Order Quality

Most Etsy sellers have positive feedback about Printful's overall order quality and fulfillment accuracy.

Print quality for apparel and posters is generally good with vibrant colors. Fabric items ship out neatly packaged.

There may be occasional print alignment issues, but the overall quality is reliable, especially at the affordable base pricing tiers.

Defective or damaged orders are reported to Printful for remakes or refunds to ensure customer satisfaction. Their support team is helpful for any issues.

Order samples yourself to proactively inspect the quality of the products you plan to sell.

Printful Pros for Etsy Sellers

Here are some of the key advantages Printful offers for Etsy stores:

- **Huge Product Selection:** Apparel, home decor, and phone cases are customized.

- **No Upfront Inventory Costs:** Orders are only printed after customers purchase so you don't have to stock items.

- **Easy Etsy Integration:** Seamless syncing with automatic order import and tracking updates back into Etsy.

- **Print-on-Demand:** No minimum orders are required so you can test new product ideas.

- **Order Fulfillment:** Printful handles printing, packing, and shipping for each order.

- **Warehousing:** Printful stores and ships products from warehouses in the US, Mexico, and Europe.

- **Mockup Generator:** Easy to create branded mockups of products to use in listings.

- **Affordable Pricing Tiers:** Caters well to new Etsy sellers on a budget.

For new Etsy shop owners, Printful eliminates huge barriers like production, inventory, and shipping to get started. Their wide selection and Etsy integration make the platform appealing.

Printful Cons to Consider

However, there are some potential drawbacks to weigh as well when assessing Printful:

- **Production Delays** - Printful has experienced delays, especially during peak sales periods, which can lead to customer complaints.

- **Lack of Control** - Rely fully on Printful's production and shipping timelines.

- **Additional Costs** - Reselling fees, shipping markups, and production costs add up. Must account for in pricing.

- **Low-Profit Potential** - After Printful costs, the profit margin per order may not be very high.

- **Can't Customize Processes** - Must adhere to how Printful has systems set up.

- **No Branding** - Printful (not your brand) will be on packaging slips and labels.

- **No Unique Products** - You can only use what's in the Printful catalog.

While Printful does have downsides like potential delays, lack of control, and branding challenges, the ease of setup and fulfillment automation benefits tend to outweigh the cons for most new Etsy sellers. It is important to carefully calculate your pricing and margins to make Printful fees don't eat up all your potential profit.

Also, you should have a plan to eventually graduate to your fulfillment and branding as your Etsy shop grows. Printful works best as an introductory solution.

Printful Product Pricing Tips

To make sure you earn a profit selling Printful products on Etsy, follow these pricing practices:

- Use the Printful price calculator to tally all base, reselling, and shipping fees per item.

- Calculate your desired profit margin per item (aim for 2-3x cost at minimum).

- Pad pricing to account for Etsy transaction fees.

- As a rule of thumb, avoid going below 2.5x-3x Printful base cost.

- Price your items just under psychologically appealing thresholds like $19.99 instead of $20.

- Offer tiered pricing like standard, premium, and luxury product versions.

Pricing appropriately is imperative. You don't want to go in the red after Printful, Etsy, and other costs.

Optimizing Printful for Etsy

Here are some tips for getting the most out of Printful as an Etsy seller:

- Order samples of your products to inspect quality firsthand.

- Compare Printful product dimensions against your shipping profiles.

- Add production time to processing times in listings.

- Set customer shipping expectations clearly in policies.

- Drive volume to lower base costs through tier discounts.

- Offer premium shipping upgrades for faster delivery.

- Use the highest print quality options your margins allow.

- Follow up on delayed orders before customers have to reach out.

Putting in work on the front and back end will enhance the customer experience and your brand reputation when using Printful.

Printify – Apparel, Mugs, Blankets, etc. (Print on Demand)

Printify is another popular print-on-demand production partner used by Etsy entrepreneurs. Like Printful, Printify allows you to design and sell customized products online while handling manufacturing and order fulfillment.

In this next section, you'll learn how Printify works, its product catalog, integrations, pricing, order quality, pros and cons, and tips for success when selling Printify products on Etsy.

Printify Overview

Printify was founded in 2015 and has become one of the largest print-on-demand companies. It is based in Latvia with over 1 million active users. Printify integrates with Etsy, Shopify, and WooCommerce.

There are no signup fees, monthly fees, or minimum orders. They offer at least 400 print providers that manufacture orders.

Print providers are located in the US, Canada, the UK, and Australia. Printify warehouse products before shipment and provide a designer tool to create mockups.

Like Printful, Printify handles printing, storing inventory, packing orders, and shipping items out when you make a sale on Etsy. This eliminates the burden of managing production and logistics.

How Printify Works

Here is an overview of how Printify's order fulfillment process works:

1. **Set up Your Etsy Shop**

   First, create Etsy product listings using the Printify mockup generator or your photos.

2. **Connect Etsy and Printify Accounts**

   Connect your Etsy store to Printify to automatically import orders.

3. **Customer Purchases an Item on Etsy**

   When an order comes through your Etsy shop, the information is transferred to Printify.

4. **Printify Manufactures and Ships Order**

   Printify will print on demand, package, and ship the order out directly to your customer.

5. **You Get Paid by Etsy**

   After Printify fulfills the order, you get paid your profits minus their fees.

By handling production and shipping, Printify allows you to focus solely on your Etsy store's design and marketing.

Printify Product Catalog

Printify offers many similar products to Printful, with a few additional options:

- **Apparel** - T-shirts, sweatshirts, leggings, hats, and socks.

- **Bags** - Backpacks, totes, drawstring bags, fanny packs, and duffel bags.

- **Home Decor** - Tapestries, blankets, pillows, shower curtains, and wall art.

- **Accessories** - Face masks, bandanas, mugs, pins, towels, and baby bibs.

- **Stickers** - Die cut, vinyl, holographic, and other specialty sticker options.

Much of the catalog overlaps with Printful. One unique aspect is Printify's stickers and a wider range of baby/kids products.

However, Printify does not currently offer some products like jewelry, phone cases, or posters. But their apparel and home goods selection is robust.

Printify Integrations

Like Printful, Printify seamlessly integrates with your Etsy store to auto-import orders. Here is the integration process:

- Connect your Etsy account to Printify's settings.

- Orders placed on Etsy flow directly into your Printify dashboard.

- Printify pushes order updates and tracking back into Etsy.

This removes the manual work of transferring orders between Printful and Etsy. New orders are sent automatically to Printify for fulfillment.

Make sure to configure your Etsy payment and shipping settings properly before linking Printify to avoid problems. Use their guides to complete the setup process properly.

Printify Pricing and Fees

When evaluating Printify, you need to account for their product pricing model and fees:

1. **Base Product Costs**

Printify products have base costs like Printful. A basic t-shirt starts at around $8.95.

2. **Fulfillment Fees**

You pay fulfillment fees per order:

- $1.99 printing fee per order

- $3.99 fixed fulfillment fee

- Individual item prep fees ($0.85 per mug, $0.35 per poster, etc)

- 7.5% shipping cost markup

These fees include labor, materials, and bundled USPS shipping. International orders incur additional fulfillment costs.

Properly factoring in fees is crucial when pricing products to earn a profit. Printify does provide discounts at higher monthly order volumes.

Printify Order Processing

Understanding Printify's production and shipping timelines helps set customer expectations:

- **24 hours** - Order received and entered into production.

- **1 to 2 days** - Manufacturing time.

- **1 to 5 days** - US order in-transit time.

- **5 to 8 days** - Estimated delivery for domestic US orders.

- **7 to 14 days** - Estimated delivery for international orders.

Expedited 1-3 day shipping is available for an added fee. Actual order processing varies based on demand fluctuations and other factors.

You can message Printify anytime on your account dashboard if an order is delayed or other issues come up.

Printify Order Quality

Most Etsy sellers have positive reviews of Printify's print quality and fulfillment accuracy.

Their multi-provider model offers good quality control across products. T-shirts and other apparel ship out neatly packaged.

Occasional issues like print misalignments may happen. Defective or damaged orders are refunded or remade.

As best practice, order samples yourself and inspect them closely. Provide feedback to Printify if any consistent issues arise with certain providers.

Overall, Printify's production quality makes it a reliable partner for Etsy product fulfillment.

Printify Pros

Here are the key advantages Printify offers for Etsy sellers:

- **Wide Product Selection** - T-shirts, home decor, mugs, stickers, and bags are customized.

- **Easy Etsy Integration** - Automatic order syncing between Etsy and Printify.

- **Print-on-Demand** - No minimum order quantity requirements or upfront inventory.

- **Global Fulfillment** - Warehouses in the US, Canada, U.K., and Australia enable quick shipping.

- **Designer Mockup Tool** - Easy to create branded mockups for listings.

- **Multi-Provider Model** - Gives added quality control across items.

- **Affordable Pricing** - Caters well to new Etsy sellers watching costs.

For new sellers without production capabilities, Printify provides an easy onboarding experience. The Etsy integration and lack of minimums make Printify a solid starting option before bringing production fully in-house.

Printify Cons to Consider

Some potential drawbacks and limitations to think through with Printify:

- **Production Delays** - Printify has faced some delays, especially around holidays. You need to set customer expectations to avoid bad reviews.

- **Hidden Costs** - You must thoroughly calculate all Printify's fees to avoid profit loss.

- **Low Margins** - After fees, the profit per order may not be very high.

- **Little Branding** - Your logo and branding don't appear on packaging and labels.

- **Lack of Control** - Adhere to Printify's production and fulfillment timelines.

- **No Unique Items** - You can only use products in Printify's catalog.

- **International Issues** - Customers may get hit with duties/taxes from international providers.

Make sure to run the numbers and account for all Printify and Etsy fees. Communicate shipping timelines clearly to customers. The automation value of Printify often outweighs the cons for new sellers.

Pricing Tips for Printify

To earn a profit on Printify orders through Etsy, keep these pricing tips in mind:

- Use their price calculator to tally all costs per product.

- Markup pricing 2.5-3x the Printify base cost at a minimum.

- Pad pricing to cover your profit margin and Etsy fees.

- Showcase premium options like upgraded materials at higher price points.

- Bundle products to increase cart value and spread fees over more items.

- Getting pricing right ensures fees don't completely eat into your margins.

Optimizing Printify for Etsy

Some best practices to optimize Printify for Etsy sales success:

- Order samples to inspect the quality of key products.

- Compare product dimensions to set shipping profiles accurately.

- Factor production time into processing times in listings.

- Set customer shipping expectations clearly in policies.

- Offer premium material upgrades at higher prices.

- Enable faster shipping options customers can select.

- Proactively communicate about any order delays.

- Follow up quickly on any damaged or defective orders.

Taking these steps enhances the buying experience.

ShineOn - Jewelry (Print on Demand)

One of the fastest-growing segments on Etsy is customized and personalized jewelry. Selling jewelry through print-on-demand services has made it easier than ever for new Etsy sellers to get started in this lucrative market without a major upfront investment.

Why Sell ShineOn Jewelry on Etsy?

Selling customizable jewelry through a print-on-demand service like ShineOn allows you to tap into this growing market on Etsy without the headaches of designing, manufacturing, or shipping physical products yourself.

Here are some of the key benefits of selling ShineOn jewelry on Etsy:

- **Huge Buyer Demand** – Jewelry is a top seller on Etsy, with customized pieces very much in vogue.

- **No Inventory or Upfront Costs** – Print-on-demand means products are made to order, so you don't need to stock any inventory.

- **Quick Fulfillment** – ShineOn handles production and shipping, allowing for fast delivery.

- **High-Profit Margins** – Markups on personalized jewelry are substantial.

- **Less Competition** – ShineOn jewelry is still relatively new on Etsy compared to other print-on-demand brands.

- **Stand-out Designs** – ShineOn offers unique pieces you won't find anywhere else.

- **Passive Income Potential** – An Etsy shop can earn money for you while you sleep.

By leveraging ShineOn's print-on-demand jewelry products and Etsy's marketplace, you can build a profitable business without major financial risk or upfront investment. Now let's look at how to set up your Etsy shop and connect with ShineOn.

Integrating ShineOn with Etsy

ShineOn doesn't currently offer direct Etsy integration, so you'll need to connect it through Shopify first. The good news is Shopify and Etsy integrate seamlessly using Zapier. Here are the steps to get set up:

1. Sign up for a free ShineOn account at shineon.com.

2. Install the ShineOn Shopify app and connect your accounts.

3. Create a free Shopify Lite plan to access Zapier and Etsy integrations.

4. Install the Zapier app on Shopify and connect your Etsy store.

5. Set up a Zapier "zap" to automatically sync ShineOn orders from Shopify to Etsy.

Once these connections are set up, you'll be ready to add products to your Etsy shop powered by ShineOn's print-on-demand fulfillment.

Choosing Your ShineOn Products

One of the best parts about ShineOn is the huge catalog of custom jewelry you can work with. Browse ShineOn's product listing to get familiar with the range of jewelry and personalization options available. Focus on pieces you feel offer the most potential based on trends and demand. Some top sellers to consider include:

- Photo engraved pendants

- Custom map necklaces

- Engraved bar necklaces

- Pet silhouette pendants

- Fingerprint jewelry

- Coordinate bracelets

- Motivational bracelets

- Birthstone rings

- Custom name necklaces

- Engraved pocket watches

Think about special occasions like weddings, anniversaries, graduations, and holidays that your products would make great gifts for. The ability to add custom engravings and designs makes ShineOn's jewelry perfect as meaningful gifts.

Take advantage of ShineOn's product customization and templates when creating your pieces. Add names, dates, photos, fingerprints, maps, and inspirational quotes to make them extra personal. This will increase the perceived value of your products.

Creating Winning Listings

Great photos and descriptions will make your Etsy listings pop. Here are some tips for creating listings that convert:

- Use all 10 image slots in your listing to showcase different angles and views. Mix in photos of your jewelry being worn.

- Write detailed, benefit-focused descriptions - tell a story and focus on how your product will make someone feel special.

- Include potential customization options in your description so customers picture how they can personalize the item.

- Consider offering bundled sets, like a necklace with matching bracelets or earrings. This boosts order value.

- Highlight occasions your product would make a perfect gift for, like birthdays, Christmas, and Mother's Day.

- Share sample customer reviews and testimonials to build trust and social proof.

- Mention fast shipping and great customer service to increase buyer confidence.

- Use relevant keywords and tags to get found in Etsy search, but avoid keyword stuffing.

Following these tips will ensure your listings look polished, highlight your products' uniqueness, and convince buyers to purchase.

Pricing Your Products Profitably

One of the most challenging parts of selling jewelry online is figuring out pricing. You want to maximize profits but still be competitive. ShineOn's base product costs range from $10-$30. Here are some pricing strategies to consider:

- Check competitor prices for similar custom jewelry on Etsy and aim for the higher end of the range. Etsy buyers expect handmade items to command a premium.

- Price your basic product at 2.5-3x the ShineOn base price as a starting point. This allows for a healthy profit margin.

- Offer tiered pricing with upgrade options like adding gold plating or diamonds to increase order value.

- Bundle items together like a necklace with matching earrings or bracelet to boost basket size. Discount the bundle slightly.

- Run occasional sales on slow-moving products, but avoid undervaluing your products.

You can always tweak your pricing over time as you assess demand and get a feel for what customers are willing to pay. The great thing about print-on-demand is you don't have to worry about margins to cover your production costs.

Driving Traffic and Sales to Your Etsy Shop

Creating amazing products is just the first step. You need to drive targeted traffic to your Etsy shop listings to start generating sales. Here are some effective marketing strategies to get your products in front of buyers:

- Promote your shop and new product listings on social media. Create visual, engaging posts showcasing your offerings. Ask existing networks to share your posts.

- Run Etsy and Google ads targeting buyers searching for terms related to custom jewelry, engraving, and personalized gifts.

- Collaborate with relevant influencers on sponsored posts and product giveaways to reach their audience. Make sure the influencers' style aligns well with your brand.

- Join Etsy teams and forums related to jewelry selling and promotions to connect with the Etsy seller community.

- Send free samples to jewelry and gift bloggers to get product reviews and build links.

- Participate in jewelry trade shows and craft fairs to make direct connections with potential wholesale buyers.

- Offer special holiday sales and discounts around peak gifting occasions like Christmas, Mother's Day, and Valentine's Day.

- Invest time in high-quality product photos and SEO optimization to improve search visibility. Update listings frequently.

- Analyze sales data to see which products and marketing channels are performing best. Double down on what works.

With consistent marketing across multiple channels, you can build steady awareness and sales momentum for your Etsy shop.

Streamlined Order Fulfillment with ShineOn

The hands-off order fulfillment provided by ShineOn's print-on-demand service makes the process easy for you as an Etsy seller. Here is the typical workflow when you receive an order:

1. Customer places orders and payments on your Etsy shop.

2. Etsy sends order info via API to your Shopify store.

3. The order syncs automatically from Shopify to your ShineOn account.

4. ShineOn prints and personalizes the jewelry item per the order details and ships directly to your customer.

5. You mark the order as complete in Etsy once ShineOn provides the tracking number.

This automated process allows you to focus on marketing and product development rather than logistics. However, providing great customer service is still essential.

Delivering Excellent Customer Service

Don't just depend on ShineOn's fulfillment and assume your job is done once the order comes in. Going above and beyond for your customers will build loyalty and word-of-mouth buzz. Here are some useful tips:

1. Send a personalized thank you message for every order.

2. Provide fast responses if a customer contacts you with any questions or concerns.

3. Follow up after delivery to make sure they are satisfied with their purchase. Ask for a review.

4. Offer express shipping upgrades for last-minute gifting needs.

5. Allow customization changes or order modifications whenever feasible.

6. Proactively notify customers about potential shipping delays due to holidays or high order volumes.

7. Include a small gift like a branded sticker in each package for a nice surprise.

8. Maintain clear return and exchange policies and make the process easy for customers.

Delivering exceptional service will help your Etsy shop stand out and earn more five-star reviews.

CHAPTER 3

OPENING AN ETSY SHOP

Once you've determined Etsy is the right sales platform for your handmade goods or vintage wares, it's time to set up shop. This process requires thoughtful preparation if you want your store to stand out in the creative marketplace. In this chapter, you'll learn key steps for launching an Etsy shop optimized for success.

Follow the tips in this chapter to design an eye-catching banner and logo that reflects your brand identity using software like Canva. You'll learn how to craft an engaging "About" page that attracts the right customers through storytelling and build product listings for high visibility and conversion rates. You'll also find guidance on configuring shipping, pricing items profitably, and purchasing mockups to kick-start your Etsy business.

Creating a Shop Banner and Logo

Your Etsy banner acts as the header image on your shop's homepage, so making a stellar first impression is vital. This visual real estate is a prime opportunity to instantly convey your brand identity. Brainstorm descriptive words and phrases about your products, brand vibe, target audience, aesthetic style, and other identity elements. List creative visual concepts, color palettes, typography styles, and motifs to bring your banner to life.

Browse banner examples from top Etsy sellers in your niche for inspiration on aesthetics, branding tactics, and balanced image-text composition. Study what makes their banners eye-catching while aligning with the brand. Compile ideas, images, and fonts into a mood board for reference while designing your header in Canvas.

Take advantage of Canvas' massive library of fonts, graphics, illustrations, and photo templates to create a visually striking banner. Blend textual and visual elements like your logo, product photos, patterns, brand colors, and typography to draw visitors in. Make sure your banner quickly communicates your essence while enticing further exploration of your shop.

Experiment with different layouts and test on both desktop and mobile. Tweak the sizing of elements and spacing until you have a polished, professional banner that represents your brand identity and sparks the crucial first impression.

Crafting an Original Logo as the Face of Your Brand

In tandem with your banner, dedicate time upfront to thoughtfully designing a logo that becomes the face of your brand. Start by sketching concepts that symbolically capture your shop's spirit and products. Incorporate popular motifs related to your niche, like hearts, nature elements, or cooking tools. You can take an abstract minimalist route using symbolic colors, lines, and typography.

Use Canvas's extensive selection of fonts, icons, graphics, and editing tools to bring your logo vision to life. Play with variations such as different orientations, taglines, and iconography until you've designed a flexible, versatile logo mark. Consider making a customizable logo kit for use across branding materials like packaging, labels, and websites.

Ensure Visual Cohesion for Brand Consistency

Carefully review your banner and logo designs together. Choose complementary colors, typography, and graphical elements to reinforce consistency. If they clash, rework either design to create a cohesive aesthetic that strengthens your brand identity across platforms.

Thoughtfully design original graphics to avoid legal issues. Do extensive proofreading to prevent undermining your perceived professionalism, and ask trusted friends for honest feedback to refine before finalizing.

Most importantly, reflect on how each design choice contributes to the customer experience and brand image you want your shop to embody. Visitors who resonate with your distinct style are much more likely to favorite your shop and purchase.

Exporting and Uploading Graphics into Your Etsy Shop

When your banner and logo files meet your refined quality standards, export high-resolution versions from Canvas. Check which dimensions precisely meet Etsy's specifications for visibility across platforms. Carefully review your graphics on both desktop and mobile before uploading them into your Etsy Shop Manager.

Displaying polished, captivating branding elevates your shop from the start. By investing time to craft designs that convey your unique identity, you signal care in how you present your brand – inspiring customer confidence. An eye-catching banner and emotive logo draw the right customers into your Etsy shop, eager to explore your carefully crafted brand environment.

Optimizing Your Etsy Shop Banner for Maximum Impact

Now that you've designed a stellar banner, optimization tactics can help maximize its visibility and clickthrough rate.

Place key information like your logo, shop name, and product photos/illustrations prominently in the upper left third of the banner - where eyes naturally gravitate first. Use contrasting colors between text and background for easy viewing. Darker, muted background colors make the lighter text pop.

Incorporate whitespace and avoid clutter. Too many competing elements overwhelm the eye. Keep text short, simple, and large enough to read on both desktop and mobile. Getting your branding, value proposition, and CTA across quickly is key.

Add catchy, benefit-focused taglines and CTAs to further guide the viewer's eye through the banner layout. Check readability on various screen sizes. Adjust scale and spacing between elements so desktop and mobile banners are equally striking.

Run A/B tests of slightly different banner versions and layouts. Analyze results over some time to guide optimization. Make sure to refresh your banner regularly to announce sales, new products, seasonal themes, or other events. This gives repeat visitors fresh visual intrigue.

Leveraging Social Media and Other Platforms to Promote Your Brand

In addition to displaying your banner and logo prominently on your Etsy shop home page, take advantage of other platforms to gain maximum brand visibility.

Add branding graphics to your email newsletter headers, product packaging, business cards, and mailing materials.

Include your logo and visual elements on your Facebook, Instagram, and Pinterest profiles to reinforce consistency across platforms.

Run a social media promotional campaign focused solely on announcing your new logo and banner launch. Share the vision and process behind your designs to further engage customers.

Look for relevant opportunities to showcase branding, like Etsy's Virtual Labs, where you can promote new product releases or redesigns.

Consistently branding yourself on and offline strengthens recognition and trust with customers, leading to more engagement and sales.

Write Your "About Me" Story

One of the most important pages on your Etsy shop is the "About" section, where you get to share your brand story and connect with potential customers on a personal level. Taking the time to craft a compelling "About Me" story has a major impact on converting visitors into loyal buyers.

Your story should provide insight into who you are as an artist/seller, what inspires your work, and why you started your Etsy business. Share your background, creative journey, and passions to form an emotional bond with your audience. The tone should be friendly yet professional to build trust and demonstrate your expertise.

Start with an Intriguing Opening Paragraph

The opening paragraph is prime real estate to capture attention and convey what makes your business special. Focus on painting a vivid portrait of your brand while highlighting your unique value and artistry.

For example:

"Hi, I'm Joanna. I left my career in finance to pursue my lifelong passion for jewelry making and founded Serenity Jewelry. My handcrafted designs reflect my Southwestern heritage and nature's calming beauty. I create meaningful pieces sustainably from my home studio in Tucson, Arizona."

This introduction establishes credibility while setting an engaging story.

Share Your Creative Journey

The next section should expand on your background and what led you to start selling on Etsy. Share when your talents first emerged and how you honed your craft over time. Key details to include:

- Childhood memories that sparked your interests.

- Art, creative, or business classes that built your skills.

- Work or hobbies where you refined your techniques.

- How and why, you chose to make a living from your art/craft.

This backstory helps customers understand the origins of your shop and establishes you as an experienced crafter with talent worth supporting.

Open Up About Your Inspirations

Give shoppers a peek into what inspires your aesthetic and motivates you as an artist. Talk about:

- Places, eras, and cultures that influence your style.

- Favorite color palettes, textures, or motifs and why you're drawn to them.

- What sparks ideas for new product lines and collections.

- Any social or environmental causes your business promotes.

This context helps customers connect with the vision behind your work on a deeper level.

Share Your Passion and Future Goals

End your story by conveying the passion that drives you and your dreams for your Etsy business. Share:

- What you most enjoy about the creative process and interacting with customers.

- How do you want your products to make others feel.

- Plans for growing your shop and offerings.

- New skills you hope to learn on your entrepreneurial journey.

This provides a sense of purpose and visibility into your long-term commitment to quality and customer happiness.

Follow Storytelling Best Practices

Adhere to some key guidelines when crafting your About Me narrative:

1. Write in an approachable, conversational tone using "I" and "you" language.

2. Keep sentences and paragraphs brief for easy skimming on mobile.

3. Break up text with photos, quotes, or other visual elements for visual appeal.

4. Share just enough details to be personal while maintaining an aura of mystery.

5. Proofread thoroughly for spelling/grammar errors before publishing.

Continuously Optimize Your Page

Treat your "About" page as a living document. Use Etsy's built-in analytics to identify phrases and stories that resonate most with visitors. Refresh content quarterly with new photos, product launches, business milestones, or progress on goals.

An engaging narrative plays a crucial role in converting site visitors into loyal, long-term customers for your Etsy shop. By taking the time to thoughtfully craft your brand story and connect on a human level, your passion and dedication will shine through. Focus on being authentic, and don't be afraid to infuse your unique personality into the story. A compelling glimpse into the origins of your business and passion for your craft will inspire trust in buyers looking for creators who genuinely care.

Listing – How to Optimize a Good Listing

Your Etsy listings are the individual pages that promote each item in your shop. Optimizing these product descriptions is crucial for making sales and standing out in search results. Follow these tips to create compelling listings to entice customers to purchase your handmade and vintage goods.

1. Choose Descriptive, Keyword-Rich Titles

The listing title is the first element buyers see and is vital for on-page SEO. Include your most important, high-traffic keywords in a title that summarizes the product and key benefits.

For example:

"Blue Floral Print Cotton Reusable Face Mask - Washable Fabric Mask with Filter Pocket"

This title optimizes search terms like "face mask," "reusable," "floral," and "cotton" while describing the color, pattern, and features. Other tips to keep in mind:

- Place your most essential keywords and phrases first

- Keep titles under 60 characters to prevent cutoff on search pages

- Use words that accurately depict the item's style, materials, colors, etc.

- Make each listing title unique to the specific product

2. Write Robust Product Descriptions

The body of your listing is where you provide all the details a buyer needs to make a purchase decision. Cover:

- Crafting process and materials used.

- Product dimensions, care instructions, and other specs.

- Visual description of colors, prints, textures, finishes, etc.

- Origin of materials, production methods, tools, inspirations.

- Your own story connecting to the item's creation.

Additionally, organically work in targeted keywords throughout your description. But avoid overstuffing - let your brand's unique voice and the product's story shine through.

3. **Include Relevant Tags**

Tags are keywords and short phrases that categorize your listing for better discoverability. Brainstorm terms buyers would use to find your item:

- Product name/category like "pillow", "vase".

- Materials like "leather", "ceramic", "acrylic paint".

- Colors like "navy", "coral".

- Styles like "boho", "mid-century", "rustic".

- Location like "San Francisco artist".

- Occasions like "weddings", "birthday gifts".

Don't go overboard, though. Etsy recommends 8-13 tags per listing. Use the most specific terms relevant to each product.

4. **Optimize Imagery**

Great photos do more than showcase your item. They also increase perceived value while conveying your brand aesthetic. Some of the best practices include:

- Leading with a crisp, well-lit main image on a clean, uncluttered background.

- Shooting flat lay, dangling, worn/used lifestyle images as applicable.

- Showing scale using props, models, or room scenes.

- Capturing multiple angles, views, details, uses, combinations, etc.

- Optimizing editing for color accuracy, brightness, and white balance.

5. Offer Variations

If your product comes in multiple sizes, colors, or styles, use Etsy's variations feature. This allows buyers to select their options before adding to the cart for a streamlined experience.

6. Enable Key Settings

Configure all available listing settings for maximum impact:

- Shipping profiles - select all that apply.

- Item details like brand, material, style, occasion, etc.

- Processing time so buyers know when to expect delivery.

- Digital downloads, customization options, etc., if relevant.

- Item location to showcase your roots.

7. Refine and Refresh Listings

Constantly analyze your listings' performance and optimize based on insights. Update underperforming content, add new photos, or improve SEO. Delete inactive listings cluttering up your shop. Introduce seasonal variations, new colors, limited editions, etc., to reward repeat visitors.

Every element of your Etsy listings - from titles to photos to tags - represents your brand and product quality. Invest time upfront in curating an exceptional experience that delights customers and drives conversions. Showcase your handmade goods beautifully while appealing to buyer search intents and behaviors. With compelling, optimized listings, you can cut through the Etsy noise and attract buyers who'll appreciate your products for years to come.

Setting Your Shipping

Setting up shipping is a key step when opening your Etsy shop. Thoughtfully chosen shipping profiles and rates ensure your customers receive purchases smoothly while keeping costs reasonable for your business. Follow this guide to configure shipping practices that meet buyer expectations and protect your profit margins.

Activate Listings for Your Geographic Region

First, indicate your shop's geographic scope in Shop Settings. Selecting your country or region ensures listings only display to buyers you can reasonably ship to. This avoids overpromising on delivery capabilities.

Determine Your Shipping Carriers

Consider which postal carriers best serve your customers and fit your operations. Popular options include USPS, UPS, FedEx, and DHL. Evaluate factors like:

- Domestic vs. international reach.

- Pickup and drop-off logistics.

- Rate competitiveness.

- Tracking capabilities.

- Insurance and lost package support.

Many sellers offer multiple carriers to provide choices like budget vs. expedited shipping. Using Etsy's integrated carriers also enables package tracking and status updates within orders.

Set Up Shipping Profiles

Etsy shipping profiles represent your packaged order dimensions, weights, and carrier options. Create separate profiles for:

- Common package sizes like envelopes, boxes (S/M/L).

- Unique products like oversize/irregular items.

- Digital downloads and no-shipping products.

Configure each one with likely dimensions, typical weight range, valid carriers, and available services (standard, express, etc.). Profiles are tweaked later as you refine them.

Calculate Affordable Rates

Determine a rate pricing for each profile that covers your fulfillment costs while remaining competitive. Calculate your expenses for packaging supplies, labor, potential product damage/losses, and carrier rates. Add a reasonable profit margin - generally 15-30% above costs.

Some sellers charge flat rates based on order size or product type. Others use table rates tied to carrier pricing. Dynamically calculated rates adjust based on order specifics. Test different approaches when starting to find the optimal balance for profitability and customer satisfaction. Update rates as carriers adjust theirs.

Provide Processing Time Estimates

Be transparent with buyers about order processing and shipping timelines. Set handling time in shop settings, like 1-3 days. List any delays related to customization or specialty sourcing.

On each listing, specify the full processing and shipping timeframe so customers know when to expect delivery. Factor in average prep time as well as transit days for your carriers. Underpromise and over-deliver to exceed expectations.

Enable Shopping Tools

Take advantage of features that improve buyer experiences and conversion:

- Free shipping guarantees over a minimum order value.

- Shipping upgrades like expedited delivery.

- Calculated rates at checkout displaying shipping cost.

- Multiple address shipping for gifts.

- Promote Shipping Perks.

- Showcase special shipping-related offers prominently across your shop and listings:

- Free shipping minimums or no minimum promotions.

- Discounts on expedited shipping options.

- Packaging/unboxing experiences like gift wrapping.

- Delivery to PO boxes, military bases, and other scenarios.

Refine as You Grow

Track pain points around shipping and modify your configurations. You can adjust profiles and rates annually based on the data you collect. Stay updated on carrier price changes. Integrate new tools to streamline packaging and label printing. Delighted customers will gladly return to a shop that delivers orders seamlessly, affordably, and quickly.

Thoughtful shipping preparation provides a polished experience while protecting your profit margin on Etsy orders. Follow this guide to configure rates, profiles, options, and tools that instill trust and loyalty in your customers. Show buyers you care through reliable, transparent delivery of every handmade and vintage item.

Pricing Your Listing to Profit

One of the most important decisions when selling on Etsy is determining pricing for your listings. Finding the optimal price point involves balancing your costs, profit goals, perceived value, and competitive landscape. Follow these steps to price your products in a way that drives sales while achieving your desired profit margins.

Calculate Your Costs Thoroughly

Start by tallying everything that goes into producing each item:

Supplies - raw materials, ingredients, packaging.

Labor - time spent designing, crafting, and processing.

Overhead - tools, equipment, studio expenses.

Fees - listing fees, transaction fees, offsite ads.

Shipping and Fulfillment - packaging, postage.

Track expenses over time to determine average costs for specific products and batches. Include both fixed and variable costs. This provides a clear baseline for the minimum pricing needed to avoid losing money.

Determine Your Profit Goals

Decide on your profit margin expectations. Common retail margins range from 30% for lower-priced commodity items to 50-60% for specialized lines. Luxury goods see margins upwards of 70%.

Consider the margin that allows you to reinvest in growing your business through better supplies, upgraded tools, marketing campaigns, etc. Price with enough breathing room to endure sales lulls or cost fluctuations.

Research Competitor Pricing

Search Etsy and other venues to see typical pricing for similar items. Compare factors like materials, quality, craftsmanship, aesthetics, brand reputation, and other differentiators.

Identify price clustering patterns signaling standard market pricing. Also, look for gaps where demand exceeds supply. Those present opportunities to command higher pricing.

Evaluate Perceived Value

Consider what tactile, visual, and emotional factors make your work worth a higher price:

- Quality materials - leather, precious metals, and fine wood.

- Specialized skills and artistry - hand carving and metalsmith.

- Custom or made-to-order personalization.

- Limited editions and short production runs.

- Surprise elements - unique specimens and combinations.

- Deep cultural heritage and handcrafted processes.

- These elements are difficult to mass produce and increase buyers' perceived value.

Run Pricing Experiments

When unsure how customers will respond to different price points, run A/B tests across similar listings. Divide them into equal groups at varied prices, ideally staying within range of competitors.

After 1 to 2 weeks, analyze conversion rates. The sweet spot with the highest sales indicates an optimal balance of value perception versus affordability.

Consider Bundling

Offer bundles and kits at an attractive combined price. This provides greater perceived savings that can justify higher individual pricing. For example, price a set of 4 printed napkins at $40 instead of $12 each.

Refresh Pricing Over Time

Revisit your pricing quarterly as costs, value perceptions, and competitive factors evolve. Increase prices gradually over time as you build a loyal customer base and reputation. Limited promotional sales can reset price expectations between increases.

Finding the right price is a process of continuous optimization. Dedicate time upfront to calculate costs and research markets. Experiment to identify price thresholds aligned with perceived value. The optimal balance between profitability and conversion will become apparent over time through data. Adjust pricing as needed to grow profit margins sustainably.

Getting Good Mockups for Your Listing

Mockups are staged product photos designed to showcase items in a lifestyle context. Using mockups in your Etsy listings can grab buyers' attention and drive sales by helping them envision using your products. Follow these tips for sourcing and styling mockup images that boost perceived value.

Evaluate Free vs. Premium Mockups

Thousands of free mockups are available to download online. While convenient, these often look generic and overused. Investing in premium mockups from Etsy or stock sites like Creative Market is worthwhile for a more elevated, custom aesthetic.

Consider purchasing collections tailored to your niche, like apparel, invitations, and wall art. Coordinated sets allow showcasing your work in a cohesive lifestyle brand vision.

Mockups with removability features make adding your designs effortless. Transparent backgrounds easily isolate just the template shape. Customizable mockups allow tweaking textures, colors, and arrangement.

Choose Mockups That Align with Your Brand Style

Select mockup scenes, props, backgrounds, and textures that reinforce your desired brand image. Rustic wood and linen textures align with a natural, homemade aesthetic. Bold, solid colors and geometric props convey modern minimalism. Showcase children's items in youthful rooms with bright colors and whimsical details.

Styling your mockups for consistency throughout your shop listings strengthens your visual identity.

Learn Photoshop to Enhance Mockups

Basic Photoshop skills allow you to customize mockups however you want. Watch tutorials on removing backgrounds, layering images, adjusting shadows and highlights, and retouching.

With practice, you can:

- Change mockup colors to coordinate with your products.

- Seamlessly insert product photos into mockup templates.

- Adjust the image size and angle to align with the mockup angle.

- Enhance details like linens, surfaces, and metallic finishes.

- Add custom graphics, text, or other branding elements.

This makes mockups feel tailored to your brand, not generic templates.

Style Mockups Thoughtfully

When digitally adding your product to a mockup, consider:

- **Scalability** – Size your design appropriately in proportion to the mockup.

- **Perspective** – Adjust the angle to match the mockup viewpoint.

- **Lighting** – Soften or brighten to coordinate with the mockup lighting.

- **Focus** – Enhance focal points like prominent text or central images.

- **Composition** – Make sure your design doesn't feel cluttered within the mockup.

- **Realism** - Add natural imperfections and wear instead of overly perfect.

These refinements help the final image feel cohesive and believable.

Use Mockups Strategically Across Listings

Avoid overusing the same mockup across too many listings. Repurpose creatively by:

- Changing up styling like linens, surfaces, and props.

- Showing alternate uses like a framed print in a living room and nursery.

- Modifying compositions and angles for visual interest.

- Pairing with different lifestyle photos across listings.

Refreshing mockups periodically keep your products' images looking current to reward repeat site visitors.

Compelling mockup photos allow Etsy buyers to picture your handmade and vintage items in real-life use. Invest in high-quality mockups tailored to your niche and style. With thoughtful styling and a dash of Photoshop magic, you can make listings feel upscale, bespoke, and appealing to your customers.

CHAPTER 4

HOW DOES SEO WORK ON ETSY?

Driving traffic to your Etsy shop requires understanding search engine optimization. In this chapter, you'll learn how SEO works on Etsy and essential tactics to improve discoverability and sales. You'll master how strategic keywords, titles, and tags can optimize your listings for relevance in search results. You'll also find out how to research the best terms and phrases to rank your products high when customers search.

By the end of this chapter, you'll be implementing key analytics to track your shop's search performance over time, and techniques to benchmark against competitors and identify new SEO opportunities. With the knowledge provided in this chapter, you can actively monitor your shop's search presence and continuously refine your metadata and content.

Tag and Title

Choosing the right tags and titles for your Etsy listings is one of the most important things you can do when setting up your shop. Tags and titles are vital for getting your items found in Etsy search, which is how most of your potential customers will discover you. Optimizing your titles and tags for search engine optimization (SEO) helps your listings appear higher in search results, leading to more views and sales.

As a new Etsy seller, you'll want to spend time brainstorming and researching keywords and phrases that customers are searching for. This ensures your items get visibility in those searches. You'll also want to incorporate those keywords naturally into your titles and tags.

Here's a closer look at how to effectively use tags and titles when opening your Etsy shop.

Tags - What They Are and Why They're Important

Tags are essentially keywords or short phrases that describe your item and what it is. They allow buyers to easily find your listings when they search relevant terms on Etsy.

For example, if you make handmade candles, some of your tags would likely be things like "candles," "home fragrance," "gift for her," etc.

The main things to know about Etsy tags:

- You can have up to 13 tags per listing. Use all 13 to cover as many relevant search terms as possible.

- Tags are single words or 2-3 word phrases. Keep them short and descriptive.

- Using more tags leads to better search visibility. Max them out for every listing.

- Reuse your most important tags across multiple similar listings to associate your shop with those terms.

- Use a mix of broad and more specific/niche tags to cast a wider net.

- Only use tags directly related to what you're selling. Don't overdo it or use spam tags.

Research the terms customers look for to help guide your choice. Look at your item title and description for other tag ideas.

Overall, optimized tags are tremendously important for getting your work discovered on Etsy. Treat them as a priority when creating new listings.

Crafting the Perfect Title

Your title is the very first thing buyers see when browsing search results. It needs to capture their attention and get them intrigued enough to click for more details.

Follow these tips for writing compelling SEO-friendly Etsy titles:

- Place your most important keywords and phrases at the beginning of the title. This gives them more weight with search engines.

- Include your main tags/keywords in the title. That reinforces their relevance.

- Keep titles short, about 60 characters or less. You want the full title to show in search results.

- Use descriptive language and specifics like colors, sizes, and materials. That lets buyers know exactly what you offer.

- Write titles in sentence case, not all caps. That makes them read more naturally.

- Add a call to action like "Buy" "Shop Now" or "Unique Handmade Gift" to encourage clicks.

- Be truthful and accurate. Don't use misleading language or include keywords not relevant to the actual item.

- Research competitors' titles to spur new ideas, but don't copy verbatim.

Along with an eye-catching product photo, a compelling title motivates shoppers to engage further. It's your first and possibly only chance to pique their interest.

Tips for Choosing Effective Tags and Titles

The goal is to select tags and build a title using words or phrases customers search for. But how do you figure out what those are? Here are some tips:

- Brainstorm terms and descriptors related to your items. What would you search to find this product?

- Use Etsy's auto-suggest feature in the search bar to reveal popular searches. Pay attention to commonly suggested phrases.

- Look at tags and titles used by top competitors selling similar items. Consider adopting their best keywords.

- Use Google's Keyword Planner or other tools to identify high-traffic search terms related to your products. Look for high-volume/low-competition keywords.

- Research hashtags popular on social media that relate to your products. Think Instagram, Twitter, etc. These can often convert to good Etsy tags as well.

- Analyze your listings' traffic analytics to see which tags and keywords are driving the most visits. Double down on those that perform well.

Taking the time to do thorough keyword research pays off big. It means your tags and titles are aligned with proven buyer searches, which translates to better visibility and more sales.

Why Accurate Tags and SEO Titles Matter to Etsy

Optimizing your tags and titles isn't just beneficial for you as a seller - it also matters to Etsy. This is because the site wants to provide the most relevant, targeted search results to its users.

When your listings are tagged and titled accurately for what they contain, it signals to Etsy that the listing is a quality match for applicable searches. The algorithm will favor that listing compared to others that may have irrelevant tags stuffed in just to try and game search placement.

In summary, accurate SEO tags and titles that genuinely reflect your products tell both buyers and Etsy itself "This listing is exactly what you're looking for!" This wins you better visibility in search results and a better experience for customers.

It's a win-win all around when you take the time to craft tags and titles tailored specifically to what makes your items special. Doing so will get you off to a great start driving traffic from day one as a new Etsy seller.

Ask Yourself These Questions to Assess Your Tags and Titles

As you work on your Etsy listings, it helps to periodically evaluate your tag and title choices by asking yourself questions like:

- Do your tags and title accurately describe your product? Or are they exaggerations?

- Are you using the keywords and phrases people are most likely searching for to find this item?

- Have you included specifics like colors, sizes, shapes, and materials in your title?

- Are your most essential keywords covered in the opening title?

- Would you find this listing easily if you were the one searching for it?

- How is your title different from competitors? Does it have a unique focus or hook?

- Is your title the optimal length? Is it readable in search results?

- Could your tags benefit from more variety? Do you need to dig deeper for niche keywords?

- Are all 13 tag slots filled out? How can you maximize them?

Regularly asking yourself questions like these ensure your tags and titles stay optimized over time. Don't be afraid to edit existing listings to refine their tags and titles as you learn more about customer search behavior.

Be Patient and Consistent

Remember, optimizing your Etsy tags and titles for search is an ongoing process, not a one-time task. It takes diligence and patience to see results.

Stay patient if your new listings don't immediately skyrocket in search during your first weeks on Etsy. It takes time for their visibility to build through factors like your shop reviews and item favorites.

Be patient when learning which tag and title adjustments resonate most with buyers for your niche. You'll narrow in on what works best the longer you sell on Etsy.

Be consistent in using keywords across multiple listings where appropriate. This repetition tells search engines, "This is really what my items are about!" which boosts relevance.

With refined SEO tags and compelling titles, your listings will capture buyer interest in no time. Those efforts pay off greatly the more listings you optimize.

Keywords Research

Keyword research is one of the most valuable things you can do when preparing to open your Etsy shop. Finding the right keywords and phrases that customers search for is key to getting your items found in Etsy search results. Optimizing your titles, tags, and listings for those keywords is crucial for driving traffic to your shop from day one.

As a new Etsy seller, you'll want to spend ample time upfront identifying your target keywords through research. This step is well worth the effort and pays off in the long run with better visibility and more sales. Here's a primer on effective keyword research and how to leverage it for your new Etsy shop.

Why Keyword Research Matters

Keyword research gives you insider insight into the specific words and phrases people enter into Etsy's search bar to find products they want to purchase. You can then align your shop and listings to strategically target those same keywords.

When you optimize for keywords that potential buyers are actively searching for, it boosts the chances of your items appearing prominently in their search results. That translates to more views, favorites, and sales.

In short, keyword research is the process of uncovering the terminology and language your target audience uses around your products. You can then "speak their language" through your Etsy SEO to get on their radar.

Without keyword research, you're just guessing about what words best describe your items. But with proper research, you're laser-focused on proven keywords that attract high buyer interest and traffic on Etsy.

How to Conduct Etsy Keyword Research

Keyword research takes some legwork, but it's a relatively straightforward process. Here are the main steps:

1. Brainstorm an initial list of potential keywords. These will be the seed keywords to build out from. Think broadly at first about words or short phrases that describe your products, brand, materials, and techniques.

2. Use the Etsy search bar to see the site's auto-fill suggestions. Pay attention to the most frequently suggested keywords and add these to your list. The auto suggestions are based on actual buyer searches.

3. Check Etsy search trends to see current popular and fast-growing searches. Look for opportunities to align with rising trends.

4. Search Google Keyword Planner and other tools to discover keyword volumes and competitiveness for your initial seed keywords. Look for high-traffic keywords that are less competitive.

5. Study competitors' listings on Etsy to identify their commonly used keywords in titles, tags, and descriptions. Consider adopting the best terms that fit your products.

6. Search hashtags used on social networks like Instagram that are relevant to your products. Popular hashtags can equate to good Etsy keywords.

7. Use keyword grouping tools to find additional keyword variations and ideas related to your seed keywords.

8. Once you've compiled a thorough initial list, narrow it down by focusing on the keywords that have the highest search volume and relevance to your specific products. Those are the terms to concentrate your Etsy SEO efforts on.

What Makes a Good Keyword?

When researching and selecting your target Etsy keywords, keep these criteria in mind:

1. **Sufficient search volume -** Enough people search for it each month for sales opportunities. Don't go after keywords searched less than 1,000 times monthly.

2. **Relevance -** Directly relates to your products or brand. Don't stuff unrelated keywords to cheat the Etsy algorithm.

3. **Opportunity** - The keyword has buyer traffic but low competition from other shops. This increases your odds of ranking well.

4. **Commercial intent** - Keywords used by people ready to purchase, not just browsing. (Ex. "buy candle wall sconces" vs. simply "candle sconces").

5. **Unique to you** - Keywords that set you apart or describe your unique niche different from competitors.

6. **Universal** - Keywords all buyers would use, not just niche subgroups. Helps cast a wider net.

7. **Exact match** - Focus on 1-3 word keyword phrases buyers are likely to search verbatim, not just concepts.

8. **Evergreen** - Relevant keywords that won't fade over time with short-term trends or seasons.

9. **Conversational** - Opt for natural language keywords, not overly technical or clunky.

Prioritize keywords hitting all or most of these criteria. Downloadable templates can help you track and narrow down your list.

Tools to Use in Keyword Research

Keyword research doesn't have to be completely manual. There are various helpful tools out there to streamline the process:

Google Keyword Planner

A free tool that shows search volumes and competitiveness data for keywords. Very useful for initial research.

Etsy Search Page

The real-time suggested keywords that auto-populate when buyers search are a great insight into current demand.

ERank

Paid tool specifically designed for Etsy keyword research including competitor analysis. Offers robust sorting and tracking.

Marmalead

Browser extension and paid subscription for in-depth Etsy keyword research. Shows competitor's top keywords.

Eranks

Lower cost paid tool with suggested Etsy keywords and niche analysis features. Good for beginners.

Soovle

A free online tool that generates keyword ideas related to your seed keywords. Good for finding additional variations.

UberSuggest

Free keyword research tool that shows monthly searches, costs-per-click, and other data.

Don't get overwhelmed by all the options. Start with free tools like Etsy Search and Google Keyword Planner to gather most of what you need. Then, try paid platforms like ERank or Marmalead for deeper competitive analysis.

How to Use Keywords on Etsy Listings

Once you've narrowed down your target keyword list, it's time to put them to use, optimizing your Etsy listings. Focus on organically incorporating keywords in:

The Title - Place your most essential 1-3 word keyword phrase near the start of the title for maximum impact.

The Tags - Fill all 13 tag slots with your most relevant keywords and phrases. Don't stuff or repeat tags.

The Description - Naturally work keywords into sentences in a conversational way. Mention them near the top.

Variation Listings - Optimize different variations of a product (like size or color) to target additional niche keywords.

Shop Sections - Include keywords relevant to your brand or product offerings in shop sections like "About".

Stuffing listings with repetitive keywords that look like spam may get your shop penalized by Etsy. Instead, work them in smoothly where appropriate.

The keywords in your titles and tags carry the most weight, so focus optimization efforts there first.

Read the performance of your keywords. Once your listings start getting traffic, you can use Etsy Stats or an app like Marmalead to assess which keywords are performing best at driving visits and sales.

Analyze this data to determine:

Which keywords have the highest conversion rates from views to sales? Double down on those in other listings.

Are your main target keywords bringing in significant traffic, or are other surprise keywords? Shift focus accordingly.

Look for rising keywords gaining more searches over recent months. Quickly optimize to capitalize on new trends.

Tweak underperforming keywords and capitalize on winners iteratively. Keyword optimization is always a work in progress as buyer searches evolve.

Mastering Keyword Research for Ongoing Success

Conducting thorough keyword research and regularly refreshing it provides incredible insight into buyer behavior on Etsy. The effort you put in upfront determines how easily shoppers find you in their searches.

Don't get intimidated by the process. Start with a few core seed keywords and expand out from there using the various free tools available.

Once your new shop launches, keep a close eye on your keyword analytics. Double down on what works well, eliminate what doesn't, and adjust to rising trends.

With the right foundation of keyword research, your Etsy shop has great chances to get discovered by buyers and start making sales much faster. It's one of the most valuable investments of effort you can make as a new Etsy seller.

Tracking

Tracking key metrics and data about your Etsy shop's performance is crucial for making smart business decisions as a new seller. The analytics and statistics available to you provide valuable insights that can significantly impact your shop's success if leveraged properly.

Keep reading to explore what types of tracking and analytics to pay attention to, and how to use them to improve your SEO and grow your new Etsy shop.

Use Etsy Stats to Track Listing Views and Sales

Etsy provides a built-in analytics dashboard called Etsy Stats that you can monitor frequently. It tracks vital metrics like:

Listing Views - Total views each of your items gets. This indicates if your SEO and promoted listings are working.

Shop Visits - Total daily and monthly views your overall shop receives. More visits mean more chances of making sales.

Sales Orders - Number of sales and revenue you're generating. The key to assessing growth and profitable products.

Traffic Sources - Where your shop views are originating from, like Etsy search, Google, social media, etc. Allows you to see what's working best at driving traffic.

Conversion Rate - Percentage of visits that convert to orders. Higher is better. Can indicate issues with product pricing, listings, etc if low.

Checking Etsy Stats daily or weekly enables you to catch any changes in these metrics quickly. You can then take actions like tweaking listings or investing more in ads for poor-performing items.

Tools like EtsyRank provide expanded statistics and analytics not available in Etsy Stats, so they're worth exploring, too. Start by making Etsy's own Stats tool part of your regular seller workflow.

Track Keyword Performance

You invested significant time researching and selecting the right keywords to optimize your listings for search. Now, you need to see which ones are driving results.

Both EtsyRank and Marmalead provide keyword-tracking tools to assess performance. You can see metrics like:

Impressions - How many times have your listings appeared in search results for that keyword? Keep in mind that the higher, the better.

Clicks - Clicks your listings get for a particular keyword. Indicates buyer interest level.

Click-through-Rate - Click-through-rate (CTR) from search impression to actual click. Higher CTR indicates your title and images are compelling.

Conversions - Number or percent of clicks on a keyword that resulted in a sale conversion. Very telling of real sales value per keyword.

Check keyword metrics weekly or monthly to see which ones have the highest ER, clicks, and conversions. Then, adjust your SEO to double down on those winning keywords in more listings. Prune any lackluster keywords dragging down performance.

Continually optimizing for your best high-converting keywords is key to maximizing the value of your Etsy SEO efforts.

Use Google Analytics for Website Tracking

If you have your website to support your Etsy shop (an increasingly good idea), you'll want to set up Google Analytics.

This free tool provides a wealth of data about traffic to your website, including:

Visitor Stats - Where they come from, their language, device, etc. That gives you the chance to understand your audience.

Acquisition - Traffic sources driving people to your site, whether organic search, social, referrals, etc. Identifies opportunities.

Behavior - What visitors do on your site, like pages visited, buttons clicked, and time on site. This helps you improve user experience.

Conversions - Key actions taken, like email signups, purchases, and downloads. This is essential for calculating the ROI of your marketing and SEO initiatives.

With Google Analytics, you have the insights needed to further boost your website traffic, serve your audience better, and expand sales beyond just your Etsy shop.

The key is looking at all this data regularly and taking action on the insights - not just setting up tracking and forgetting about it. Assign time at least weekly to analyze trends and metrics.

Audit Listings Frequently

Beyond sales and traffic numbers, take time to regularly audit the overall SEO health of your Etsy listings.

Every few months, do an audit examining factors like:

Title length, keyword placement.

Use of all 13 tag slots with relevant keywords.

Number of quality photos and keywords in descriptions.

Introduction of new product variations.

Adoption of new trends and keywords.

Removal of outdated listings.

Regular auditing ensures you catch any issues early before they impact sales long-term. It also prompts you to improve and evolve listings continually over time as you learn more.

An audit may reveal listings that need renewed attention, like boosting keywords for flagging items or optimizing tags in old products. Treat your listings like a living organism that constantly needs care.

Learn from Your Top Performers

Your top-performing listings by views and sales provide great clues about what's working well.

Analyze the titles, tags, photos, and descriptions on these listings to understand why they resonate so strongly with buyers.

Look for elements you can replicate in new listings, like:

Title keywords and formats that grab attention.

Specific tag themes that buyers respond to.

Photo angles and props that convert well.

Descriptions focused on benefits and emotions instead of just specs.

Let your top sellers become templates for how to create more high-converting listings. Study and apply what makes them so popular.

Tracking Provides the Data You Need to Improve

Making data-driven decisions about your Etsy shop based on performance tracking and analytics gives you a big advantage as a new seller.

Instead of guessing, you'll know what's working well to attract buyers and make sales. You'll quickly see when metrics dip so you can take corrective actions before long-term impact.

Make a habit of closely following the analytics available to you. Then, use those insights to actively refine your Etsy SEO and shop strategy on an ongoing basis.

The combination of analytics-focused tracking and continuous improvement will serve your new Etsy business well in its foundational months.

Ranking

Achieving a high search ranking for your Etsy listings is vital for generating traffic and sales as a new shop. Where your items are placed in the search results pages when potential customers search relevant keywords determines whether they will ever find and view your products.

Optimizing your title formatting, tags, descriptions, and overall shop for Etsy's search algorithm gives you the best chance of ranking well and getting your listings visibility in those critical searches. Consistently appearing high on the first couple of pages of results for your target keywords leads to exponential growth in the number of eyes that will visit your shop.

Focus First on Crafting Optimal Titles

The first place to focus your time and effort when optimizing Etsy listings for better search ranking is your title. The title has the biggest influence on how Etsy's search algorithm scores and ranks your listing for a given keyword search.

Some best practices to follow for optimizing your Etsy listing titles:

Place your single most important, relevant keyword phrase right at the beginning of the title. Having it earlier in the title gives it more weight and priority in the algorithm's ranking factors.

Keep titles relatively short and easily readable, ideally around 50-60 characters or less if possible. You want the full title easily readable in the condensed search results.

Use compelling, interest-grabbing wording in the title to intrigue shoppers. Work your keywords in smoothly - don't just cram them in awkwardly.

Avoid stuffing multiple keyword phrases in a disjointed way. Make sure it flows and reads like a title should.

Use normal title capitalization, with just the first words capitalized rather than everything in caps. All caps can reduce clickability.

Make every word count. No fluff or filler. Keep it tight.

Taking the time to perfect your titles for each Etsy listing with the right keyword optimization gives you a real advantage in achieving those coveted first-page search result placements.

Maximize Your Use of Listing Tags

After the title, tags are the second most important element to focus on for improving Etsy search ranking. Tags essentially function as descriptive meta keywords that complement and build on your title. Some guidelines around optimizing tags:

Fill out all 13 available tag slots for each of your Etsy listings. The more relevant keywords you use, the better your visibility.

Choose your tags strategically based on keyword research reflecting what terms people are searching for related to your niche and products.

Your tags should succinctly describe what your item is. But also consider throwing in some less obvious niche tags, too.

Try repeating some of your most relevant 1-3 word tags that best describe your overall brand and offerings across multiple similar listings. This repetition helps associate those keywords with you.

With 13 slots available, tags allow you to incorporate a nice diversity of keyword phrases to capture a wider range of potential searches. Thus, maximize your use of tags on every listing.

Craft Descriptions That Captivate

While your description doesn't factor directly into search ranking as much as titles and tags, take time to craft it well, as it can help in small ways. As the long-form sales pitch for your item, you want the description to:

Expand on your title and tags with vivid details that bring the listing to life. Don't forget to provide the full visual story.

Naturally, incorporate some of your relevant keywords early on in the first paragraph or two. But don't just cram them in awkwardly - keep it engaging.

Highlight what makes your particular creative work unique or special in some way, and share your creative process or backstory.

Speak to the benefits, emotions, and meaning your item stirs in those who use/display it. Make it personal.

Use conversational language and specifics like colors, materials, techniques, etc., to help the buyer envision it.

Descriptions hold more SEO weight over time as your shop accumulates more sales and customer engagement. For new shops, focus on tightening titles and tags.

Naturally, Sprinkle Keywords Everywhere

Don't overlook working great keywords naturally into any other listing elements where you can fit them.

For handmade items especially, be sure to list out all the materials used. This provides opportunities to organically incorporate more niche keywords.

In your Etsy shop sections like "Shop Story", "Announcements", and "About", sprinkling relevant keywords can benefit search ranking a bit by associating terms with your brand story.

Optimize each variation listing like different sizes or colors slightly differently with unique keywords tailored to it.

Use descriptive captions on your photos that seamlessly work in keywords where relevant.

Be helpful and creative with keyword incorporation throughout your listings.

Choose Photos That Convert Clicks

Compelling product photos won't directly influence search ranking, but they will powerfully impact your click-through rate from search result listings pages. More clicks signal relevance to Etsy, indirectly elevating your rankings over time.

Some tips for product photography:

Highlight your product by shooting it clearly as the central focus, with minimal background distractions.

Shoot straight on instead of using odd angles. Crop in tightly on the product details.

Use bright, even, flattering lighting. Avoid shadows, glares, etc.

Pick lifestyle images that visualize how a real customer would use and appreciate the item.

Maintain a consistent editing style and filters across your shop listings for a polished brand image.

Investing in professional-quality photos can massively boost your clicks and conversions from search traffic.

Follow Etsy's Guidelines Diligently

To avoid jeopardizing your shop's standing, diligently follow Etsy's published guidelines around acceptable SEO practices. Never try shortcuts like cramming listings with repetitive keywords just to game search placement, as you may get penalized.

Other big violations include using trademarked terms you don't have rights to, copying competitor content, inaccurate titles or keywords, or anything else that misrepresents your items.

Read Etsy's SEO guide thoroughly and stay within their best practices recommendations to prevent issues.

Refine and Monitor SEO Over Time

Don't expect your brand new shop's listings to suddenly skyrocket to page 1 search rankings overnight. It takes consistent effort over the first couple of months for Etsy's algorithm to assess and rank your new listings well.

Instead of obsessing over daily rank fluctuations, maintain a patient, long-term focus on continuously improving your SEO.

Use Etsy Stats, Google Analytics, ERank, or Marmalead to monitor your listings' search performance over time.

Identify listings consistently ranking on page 1 for your target keywords and optimize new listings accordingly based on what's working.

For listings stuck on later pages, refresh elements like titles, tags, and descriptions to bump them up.

CHAPTER 5

HOW TO GET YOUR FIRST 100 SALES

Reaching 100 sales is a pivotal milestone. In this chapter, discover proven strategies to hit this target and build momentum. Learn how targeted Etsy ads can drive interested traffic to your listings. Understand the power of social proof and how to get honest reviews that build trust and credibility.

Leverage social media to authentically connect with your audience and promote products. Run special limited-time promotions like sales and countdowns to incentivize buying. The knowledge in this chapter empowers you to actively generate sales, delight customers, and move your shop toward ongoing profitability.

Consider Running Etsy Ads to Drive Traffic

Opening an Etsy shop is an exciting first step, but getting those initial sales is very challenging when you're just starting. Consider launching Etsy ads soon after opening your shop to help drive momentum during the critical launch phase.

You may be hesitant to spend money on advertising before you have made any sales. However, investing a small everyday budget into Etsy ads can kick-start your shop's success. Etsy provides an easy-to-use advertising platform to get your products in front of interested buyers right away.

Starting ads early takes advantage of the "new shop boost" that Etsy's algorithm gives to help new sellers. Promoting your listings right out of the gate can convert initial traffic into sales more quickly. Be patient and consistently fund your ads for at least the first few weeks to give them a chance to work.

Create Compelling Ads Showcasing Your Best Products

Carefully select which of your product listings to turn into ads. Choose your absolute best sellers that exhibit your unique skills and styles. For a new shop, advertised listings should be your highest quality pieces that will make a great first impression.

Craft engaging ad copy to capture attention quickly and convey why shoppers should purchase from your shop. Call out your creative process, quality, or other points of differentiation. Use compelling wording like "handcrafted with love" or "modern designs" as appropriate to your products.

Make sure your ad photos are top-notch since they have to stand out from the crowd. Review Etsy's tips for taking great product shots. Invest in a lightbox and camera if needed. Crisp, well-lit, high-resolution images on white backgrounds tend to convert better.

Track Performance to Optimize Your Ads

Pay close attention to how your ads are performing using Etsy's analytics tools. Review which keywords and specific product listings generate clicks, impressions, and sales.

Use these insights to refine your ads. Make changes to improve results over time, such as adjusting your keyword targets, bidding, budget, headline, or photo. Aim for a cost-per-click around $0.15-$0.20 as a reasonable starting point.

Be consistent in gathering this data and making incremental improvements. Over time, you will discover what works best to promote your unique products and attract buyers. Fine-tuning your ads is key to maximizing your ad spend.

Benefit from Increased Visibility in Search Results

In addition to ad placements, Etsy advertising can increase your visibility in organic search results. When a buyer searches keywords related to your items, promoted listings appear higher alongside other search results.

This gives you a much better chance of being discovered by potential customers browsing for products like yours. The higher positioning drives more traffic to your shop and products. So, consider your ad spend an investment in increased exposure.

Monitor your click-through rate from promoted vs. organic listings to gauge the impact. Over time as you build reviews, your organic visibility may increase, allowing you to scale back ads. But initially, ads are crucial to getting found faster.

Promote on Social Media to Reach Your Audience

Expanding your promotional efforts beyond Etsy ads is important when starting. Leverage social media platforms like Instagram, Facebook, and Pinterest, where your target buyers are spending time.

Create eye-catching social posts showcasing new products, studio sneak peeks, or your creative process. Engage with your niche community to build connections. Use relevant hashtags and tags to get on the radar of ideal customers.

Consider small investments in targeted social ads on these platforms to complement your Etsy ads. But focus on cultivating organic engagement for the long term. Partner with aligned makers or influencers to broaden your reach through collaborations like giveaways.

Collaborate with Fellow Makers to Expand Your Reach

Speaking of collaborations, partnering with complementary makers or influencers can provide an audience boost. Explore product trades to cross-promote your shops.

Join forces for social media giveaways where you gift products to one winner. Sponsors gain new followers and awareness. You could also sponsor or be a vendor at local craft fairs together.

Getting involved with an Etsy team in your region or niche helps, too. Brainstorm creative ways to collaborate that feel natural for your brand. Avoid overly commercial partnerships that could alienate your audience.

Get an Honest Review for Social Proof (Friend or Family)

However, thoughtfully written, authentic feedback has much more influence on potential buyers than generic, overly positive praise. Take the time upfront to get quality reviews from connections who have genuinely purchased from and interacted with your new shop.

Make a Real Sale, then Request a Review

Start by having a crafty friend or family member who appreciates your style of work buy something from your shop that they would genuinely use and enjoy. Make sure they organically like the specific item they purchase. After they receive their order, politely request they leave an honest, thoughtful Etsy review describing their real experience as a buyer.

Give them some guidance and suggestions to mention more helpful details beyond just "great product, great seller" in their review. Ask them to mention specific things like the packaging, shipping speed, overall quality, and uniqueness of the item, how it fits their needs and style, and their full experience purchasing from your shop, from browsing to unboxing. Reviews that include more context, substance, and specifics come across as far more authentic, trustworthy, and ultimately influential to potential customers who read them.

Offer to Reciprocate with a Thoughtful Review

In exchange for their time and genuine review, make sure to purchase something yourself from their Etsy or small business. Then, make the effort to provide an equally thoughtful, detailed, and honest review describing your experience as a customer. Reciprocity can provide extra motivation for them to give your shop a review, as long as the feedback both ways is completely authentic and not exaggerated or paid for.

Avoid Paid or Inauthentic-Seeming Reviews

It's against Etsy policies to pay someone for a positive review or feedback. Trades done to artificially inflate review numbers by scratching each other's backs can seem disingenuous and get reviews removed by Etsy if discovered. While it is tempting to take shortcuts, genuine, organic feedback will always carry more weight and credibility in the eyes of your potential buyers.

Embrace Constructive Criticism

Be gracious if you request a review from someone close to you, and they end up sharing polite but critical or negative feedback. Avoid getting defensive, and instead apologize sincerely, offer them a replacement product or refund graciously, and learn from their perspective. They may even update their review to be more positive if you handle it with care and provide extraordinary service.

Continue Requesting Quality Reviews

As you make more sales to unconnected customers, politely ask happy buyers to leave honest Etsy reviews, mentioning specific details they enjoyed about their purchase. Reviews that provide more thoughtful context beyond just generalized praise build your credibility so much more as a new shop owner. Even just two or three quality reviews from real customers establish far more trust and confidence in your shop as you start.

Follow Up Personally with Select Customers

Once your Etsy shop begins to grow, you likely won't have the capacity to get in-depth reviews from every single buyer. Instead, thoughtfully follow up with customers who you feel would be most likely to leave thoughtful, authentic feedback based on their purchases from you and overall interactions with your shop.

Consider offering loyal repeat buyers or customers who bought higher priced items a discount on a future purchase in exchange for their time reviewing a product they bought previously.

The Power of Reviews from Those You Know

In summary, just two or three honest, detailed reviews during your Etsy shop's early days can tremendously elevate the sense of social proof, trust, and confidence for potential customers browsing your new shop. Focus on selectively getting authentic feedback from friends, family, and customers, most likely to provide thoughtful, quality reviews instead of pursuing the highest quantity possible.

Patiently build up genuine reviews over the first few months, along with excellent customer service, stellar product photos, smart digital marketing tactics, and frequently adding new product listings. Before long, you'll become an established name on Etsy in your niche.

With determination, consistently delivering quality products and experiences, and crafting a cohesive brand presence, you'll gradually get honest reviews from satisfied customers. In turn, that hard-earned social proof will drive more organic traffic and sales as your Etsy shop grows. Stay relentlessly focused on your creative passion, and success will follow.

Promote on Social Media

One of the first steps in promoting your Etsy shop on social media is to set up dedicated business profiles on each platform you want to use, such as Instagram, Facebook, and Pinterest. Keep your shop name consistent across these profiles to make it easy for interested buyers to find and remember you.

Craft an engaging bio for each profile that shares a bit about you, your business, and what makes your products special. Include relevant hashtags like #etsyseller, #handmade, or specific terms related to your niche. This helps people discover you when browsing those tags.

Showcase Your Products with High-Quality Photos

Populating your feeds with eye-catching product photos is key to making sales from social media. Shoot arranged, styled images that make your items shine. Get creative with lighting, backgrounds, props, and editing to showcase your products in a lifestyle context.

Post product photos with details like name, price, and Etsy shop link. Share new items when you list them. Post works-in-progress or behind-the-scenes sneak peeks to give customers a window into your process.

Engage with Your Niche Regularly

Interact genuinely with others in your niche by commenting on posts and responding to comments. Have real conversations to build relationships with potential buyers and fellow makers. Being helpful and sharing value earns trust.

Stay on top of engaging with your content and followers, too. Respond quickly to questions, comments, and messages. This level of care helps convert social media followers into customers.

Leverage Relevant Hashtags

Strategically use hashtags in your posts so those interested in your niche can organically find you when browsing tags. Research popular hashtags used in your category, like #knitting, #handmadejewelry, #quilting, etc, and include a few relevant ones per post.

Experiment to identify the best hashtags to reach your audience. Refine your hashtag strategy over time based on engagement and clicks generated. You just need to avoid excessive hashtag stuffing that looks like spam.

Run Contests and Giveaways

Occasional social contests or giveaways are a great way to build awareness and followers. Offer a small gift certificate or free product from your Etsy shop. Ask entrants to like your page, follow you, tag friends in the comments, or share your post publicly to enter.

Announce the winner publicly once the contest ends. This generates excitement while expanding your audience. Just don't overdo giveaways that come across as desperate.

Consider Small Social Ads

Placing inexpensive Facebook and Instagram ads allows you to reach more potential buyers. You can target your ads based on demographics, interests, and behaviors to hone in on your ideal audience.

Start with just $5-10 per day while testing ad performance. Use compelling images, minimal text, and clear calls to action. Monitor clicks, engagement, and sales to optimize future ads.

Track Performance and Refine Your Approach

Pay attention to the engagement and sales each of your social platforms drives. Review analytics like engagement rates, clicks, follows, and shares.

Take note of which posts and strategies perform best. Refine your approach over time to maximize results on each platform. Play to the strengths of each based on your audience's behavior.

Drive Traffic to Your Etsy Shop

Your social media presence ultimately exists to drive traffic to your Etsy shop. Link to your store from social profiles and promote new products, sales, and announcements.

Remind followers frequently to shop the link in your bio. Collaborate with aligned makers to cross-promote each other's Etsy shops and products.

Consistency and Patience Are Crucial

Growing an audience and presence on social platforms takes immense consistency and patience. Post regularly, engage daily, and stick with what works long-term. Sales and followers will steadily grow over time.

Don't get discouraged by low engagement initially. Organic reach takes time and effort to build. With persistence and providing value, your social channels will become vital sales drivers.

The Value of Social Selling

Leveraging social media provides immense value for establishing your handmade business. Use it to share your brand story, foster relationships, and drive ongoing traffic and sales.

With compelling content, meaningful engagement, and persistence, your social platforms will help propel your Etsy shop's success. Make social selling a regular part of your marketing approach.

Special Promotion - Sales Countdown

Temporary discounts or bundle deals can help drive coveted initial sales when first opening your Etsy shop. Limited-time promotions create a sense of urgency and excitement to purchase from your newly launched business.

Plan the Details in Advance

Before launching your first promotion, decide the specifics in advance so you can easily announce and market it - which listings you'll discount or bundle, the percentage/dollar amount off, the precise period or sale duration, any minimum spend, or quantity thresholds. Consider a roughly week-long 25% off site-wide sale as a sensible starting point, then you can perfect your approach over time.

Brainstorm creative bundles, like offering a set of coordinating products together at a bundled price or adding a free matching piece with a higher-priced item. Unique savings opportunities beyond a basic site percentage off can sweeten the appeal of your deals.

Build Excitement and Scarcity

When marketing your sales promotion, aim to create consumer FOMO - fear of missing out. Note the limited time frame or sale end date prominently in your listings and product descriptions. Use countdown timers or graphics showing days remaining to elevate the urgency to shop before the deal disappears. Suggest limited quantities are available to prompt quicker purchase decisions.

Email marketing through Mailchimp, social media giveaways, digital ads, and your Etsy shop announcements can all raise awareness leading up to your sale launch. But avoid announcing too far in advance - you want to pique interest without allowing shoppers to lose momentum. One week of strategic buildup is often ideal.

Refine Your Listings for Maximum Impact

In preparation for your promotion, take time to refine your shop's product listings - especially those you plan to spotlight or bundle during the sale. Make sure you are set up for success by having the most compelling and conversion-friendly listings ready to go with:

- Attention-grabbing titles and detailed descriptions.

- High-resolution, high-quality photos, and other multimedia.

- Appropriate and descriptive tags, categories, and keywords.

- Competitively priced items and sensible calculated shipping rates.

- Styled lifestyle images that inspire.

- Available variations are displayed to offer choices.

- Clear sizing or design customization options.

You want to put your absolute best and most enticing listings forward to make the most of your temporary sale spotlight.

Amplify Reach with Advertising

Consider placing targeted Etsy and social media advertisements to increase visibility and exposure for your limited-time shop promotion. You can create PPC ads specifically promoting your discounted products or bundle deals. Or target relevant seasonal keywords and audiences who may be newer customers.

Closely monitor the performance of your ads throughout the promotion. Watch for conversion rates, cost per click, and return on ad spend metrics. Then pause any underperforming ads and build upon the wording, imagery, or targeting that proves most effective at driving traffic and sales.

Leveraging advertising helps cut through the competitive noise and positions your shop promotion in front of fresh new buyers. The temporary investment is well worth it to kick-start initial momentum and establish your shop.

Track Performance and Optimize

Throughout the duration of your countdown sale or special promotion, diligently analyze Etsy analytics and other performance metrics. Monitor your daily and overall sales totals, traffic to your shop, bounce rates, average order values, conversion rates, top-selling items, and any other insightful data.

Use these learnings to identify your most in-demand products, most effective marketing tactics, ideal bundle deals, and average discounts. Then, refine future limited-time promotions to build upon what worked best, reduce what didn't, and ultimately convert even more shoppers into delighted customers.

Focus on Providing Exceptional Service

During the flurry of activity that comes with sales promotions, maintain high standards for customer service. Quickly fulfill orders, ship items promptly, and proactively communicate with buyers at every step. Resolve any issues, complaints, or returns with urgency.

With permission, politely ask satisfied customers to leave positive Etsy reviews of both their purchased products and their overall buying experience. This helps build credibility through social proof that will benefit your shop well after the promotion ends.

Aim for customers to be so thrilled with their orders and service that they can't wait for your next sale!

Follow Up and Build Relationships

Once your special promotion concludes, follow up with customers who purchased in a personal, authentic way. Send exclusive discounts or special offers on future purchases based on their initial order.

Thank them sincerely for their support and business through your launch promotion. Suggest additional items in your shop they may like based on their purchase history and style preferences. Invite them to follow your Etsy shop and creative journey on social media, or sign up for email updates through your newsletter list.

Nurturing these initial customer relationships drives critical repeat business, word-of-mouth referrals, and organic shop growth after a promotion.

Continue Strategic Promotions

Instead of being just a launch strategy, consider making sales promotions an ongoing tactic with your Etsy marketing approach. Run regular sales around major holidays, seasons, or other special occasions throughout the year.

Limited-time savings give existing customers extra incentive to purchase again. Just be careful not to overuse site-wide discounts that may erode the perceived value of your products and brand. Find the optimal balance that sustains profitability while using promotions to strategically spur activity.

Promote Smarter, Not Cheaper

Leveraging limited-time sales, special bundles, and countdown deals is extremely effective when initially launching your Etsy shop to drive momentum. Resist simply discounting products across the board. Instead, promote strategically - call attention to your very best items, combine gifts with higher-priced purchases, display competitive shipping rates, and convey the outstanding customer experience buyers can expect.

With preparation and persistence, sales promotions will become a key ingredient in your marketing arsenal as you establish your Etsy shop without having to resort to extreme discounting.

CHAPTER 6

MANAGING YOUR ETSY BUSINESS

Running a successful Etsy shop requires diligent behind-the-scenes management. This chapter provides strategies to steer your business through inevitable challenges. You'll learn constructive ways to respond to negative reviews and build customer trust, the best practices for handling copyright claims if your work is questioned, and how to implement a system to communicate promptly and professionally with customers at every stage.

Applying this knowledge empowers you to turn issues into opportunities to improve processes and showcase your commitment to quality customer service. Savvy management and policies make your shop more reputable to Etsy and future buyers.

You can provide a positive brand experience that drives repeat purchases and sustained growth by dedicating time to sharpening your customer service and issue resolution skills. Use the lessons in this chapter to confidently manage your Etsy shop through ups and downs while keeping your passion alive.

Bad Customer Reviews

Opening an Etsy shop is an exciting way to turn your crafting or artistic skills into a small business. However, managing an Etsy shop comes with challenges, including the occasional bad customer review. Getting a negative review is upsetting, but there are constructive ways to handle it while maintaining your shop's reputation. Keep reading for tips on responding professionally, learning from feedback, addressing issues, and focusing on your quality customer relationships.

Don't Take Bad Reviews Personally

It's understandable to feel disappointed or even hurt by negative feedback about your beautiful handmade creations. Try not to let your emotions get the better of you. Angry responses or retaliation will only make the situation worse.

The customer likely didn't intend their review as a personal attack, even if it felt that way. Take a step back, take a few deep breaths, and respond calmly once you've gathered your thoughts. You worked hard on your product, and one person's opinion doesn't determine your skill or artistry.

Respond Professionally and Constructively

Once you've had time to process the review, craft a professional response that addresses the customer's concerns without being defensive. Thank them for taking the time to provide feedback and offer your sincere apologies. If they bring up specific issues like sizing, quality, or inaccuracies, address those points directly and non-confrontationally.

Let them know you will take steps to improve moving forward. Your response lets future customers see you take feedback seriously and are committed to making things right. If the bad review was factually incorrect or abusive, you can report it to Etsy for removal.

Learn From Negative Reviews

Try looking at bad reviews as an opportunity for growth instead of a sign of failure. Is there something you can improve about your product, listing details, packaging, or shipping timelines based on the feedback? Even unfair or unrealistic expectations can teach you about managing customer relationships.

Develop a process for reviewing negative feedback to identify areas in your Etsy shop that could get better. Ask a friend to audit your product objectively. Evaluate whether you need to adjust your policies, communication style, quality control, or product descriptions. Let bad reviews better your business rather than discourage you.

Address Issues Quickly and Completely

If a negative review points out a real problem with an order, take steps immediately to make it right. Contact the customer to apologize sincerely and offer a resolution like a replacement, refund, or credit. Make sure to follow up to confirm they are now satisfied.

Handling issues swiftly and completely shows you stand behind your work and care about your customers' experience. Negative feedback is much less likely to damage your shop's reputation if you fix mistakes proactively. If the issue was an unfortunate one-off, reviewers will see your dedication to excellent customer service.

Focus on Your Quality Relationships

It's easy to obsess over a negative review, but remember that one bad experience does not reflect the entirety of your shop. You likely have regular customers who love your work and are completely satisfied. Focus your energy on continuing to nurture those relationships through excellent service and high-quality products.

Their positive experiences outweigh the singular bad review. Continue providing the same level of care and attention that built your loyal customer base. If someone is satisfied enough to leave positive feedback, you are doing many things right. Let that motivate you to keep improving.

Maintain Reasonable Expectations

With enough sales volume, even the most successful Etsy shops will inevitably get some bad reviews. You cannot please every customer or control perceptions. Some negative feedback will be unreasonable or even false. While striving for complete customer satisfaction is important, have realistic expectations.

Setting perfectionist standards could mean taking criticism too personally. Focus on the positive feedback as well and keep perspective on how the majority of your customers are happy. Don't let isolated negative experiences overshadow your shop's overall success.

A thoughtful response and learning mindset can help bad reviews make you a stronger Etsy seller. By addressing issues promptly, improving your policies and practices, and focusing on your quality customer relationships, negative feedback does not harm your shop's reputation.

Maintain reasonable expectations, keep growing your skills, and provide excellent service to nurture your loyal customer base. With your dedication to the customer experience, you can manage the occasional bad review while running a thriving handmade business.

Handling Copyright Claims

As an Etsy seller, you put love and effort into making unique, creative products for your shop. However, if your items infringe on someone else's copyright, you could face legal claims. Getting a copyright infringement notice is worrying, but handling it properly is key. With some diligence and care, you can steer clear of copyright troubles while running your handmade business.

Learn About Copyright Law

To avoid accidental copyright infringement, get educated on what intellectual property is protected. Copyright covers original works like art, photographs, books, song lyrics, and digital designs. It gives the creator exclusive rights to reproduce, distribute, and sell their work. Using someone else's protected content without permission violates their rights.

However, copyright law has exceptions for "fair use" like commentary, parody, education, and minor samples. Also, common shapes, fonts, and color palettes are not protected. Take time to understand what is and isn't legal to use in your products. Reference official resources like the United States Copyright Office website instead of making assumptions. Having this knowledge will help you stay within your rights.

Audit Your Shop Carefully

Conduct a thorough audit of your Etsy shop and product listings to catch any potential copyright issues. Carefully examine your item descriptions, photos, and any digital materials for copyrighted content. Scrutinize your use of song lyrics, book passages, movie quotes, artwork, and photographs.

Take down anything questionable and avoid reusing unverified materials. Removing infringing content before receiving a claim shows good faith. Regularly double-check new listings as well and discontinue the use of reused templates, mockups, or design elements unless verified as safe. Ongoing vigilance will prevent headaches down the road.

Seek Permission When Unsure

If you want to legally incorporate copyrighted materials, seek explicit permission from the owner first. Many creators will grant you a license for a fee. Proactively asking shows you respect creators' rights and understand copyright law. Keep written documentation of any licenses purchased in case a dispute arises later.

Don't rely on verbal permission or assume lack of response is consent. Unauthorized use puts your shop at risk, even if unintentional. When in doubt, leave it out or use materials verified as copyright-free instead. Protect yourself and your hard work by doing due diligence.

Respond Politely and Promptly

If you do receive a copyright infringement notice, remain calm and courteous in response. Thank the claimant for bringing it to your attention, and do not argue. Quickly removing flagged content and issuing an apology looks better than insisting your use was legal.

Let them know you are taking immediate action to resolve the issue. Even if you believe your case qualifies as "fair use", a legal battle will only increase costs and headaches. You have an incentive to make compliance easy. Also, promptly notify Etsy of any infringement notices you receive from rights holders.

Fix Violations Thoroughly

After a copyright claim, immediately stop selling and pull all related listings that include the protected content. Remove the material completely instead of altering products to toe the line. Changing a few words of song lyrics or using Photoshop to alter an image slightly could still be an infringement.

Don't take half-measures that prolong the dispute or leave you vulnerable to repeated claims. Destroy all physical inventory and marketing materials featuring the content as well. Reshoot product photos using only original or licensed elements. A complete removal shows you respect trademarks and are committed to following the law.

Be Transparent with Customers

When listings suddenly disappear after an infringement notice, customers may be confused or unhappy about not receiving purchases. Explain why you cannot provide the original item, but don't disparage the claimant. Offer shop credit or a comparable substitute product at their discretion.

Making the situation right demonstrates your brand's integrity. Reach out to previous buyers who purchased the infringing products, too, and offer replacements or refunds. Even if they are satisfied, they should know there is an issue. Handling matters transparently maintains your reputation and builds customer loyalty despite the difficult situation.

Move Forward Constructively

An infringement claim feels like a setback, but don't let it permanently discourage or sabotage your Etsy shop. Learn from the experience and make constructive changes to prevent repeating issues. Follow up by expanding your knowledge of copyright law and best practices.

Invest time into developing unique products using only original or licensed materials. Create your illustrations, product photos, fonts, and color schemes Establish tighter inventory controls and implement review procedures for new listings. With care and effort, your shop can recover and thrive without legal shadows overhead.

Maintain Perspective

As challenging as they are, occasional copyright claims are a normal business risk. With millions of Etsy listings, some unintentional infringements will slip through. It does not make you a bad or illegal business. You now understand where things went wrong and can improve. Don't take claims personally or over-interpret their severity.

Maintain perspective by focusing on all the happy customers you've served legally over the years. Keep providing quality products and services. In time, this will become just one learning experience out of many running your creative small business.

Copyright disputes are stressful, but handling them professionally demonstrates your values. Avoid potential issues by educating yourself on intellectual property law. Seek permissions and conduct thorough audits of your listings.

Address claims politely, comply fully by removing content, and be transparent with customers. Make constructive changes moving forward to refocus on original creations. With diligence and care, your Etsy shop can thrive in harmony with copyright protections.

Communicate with Your Customer

As an Etsy seller, providing excellent customer service is crucial for your shop's success. An essential part of good service is timely communication. Responding promptly to questions, custom orders, issues, and reviews builds trust and loyalty. On the other hand, leaving customers hanging damages your reputation.

Respond ASAP within Reason

Customers appreciate fast replies, so respond as soon as possible when you receive a message. Quick answers signal you are attentive to their needs, while delayed responses look lazy or indifferent. Set up notifications and check for Etsy messages at least every day if full-time or every couple of days if part-time.

Reply immediately if available, or by the end of the day if you're busy. Resist overcommitting to instant replies if it's not feasible long-term. Find a sustainable pace that balances responsiveness and availability. Give yourself some flexibility for when life interrupts.

Set Clear Expectations

Be upfront in your shop policies or FAQs about when customers can expect replies. "I aim to respond within 24 hours" or "Messages received weekends will be answered Monday" sets a timeline they can anticipate.

Avoid promising unachievable standards like instantaneous responses. Also, indicate any extended periods when you are unavailable. Managing expectations prevents misunderstandings and frees you from constant pressure.

Notify Any Delays

If an unusually busy period or situation will delay your response time, notify shoppers proactively via an announcement. Apologize for any inconvenience and share when you will resume typical reply speeds. For longer absences, set your shop to vacation mode.

Follow up individually with customers awaiting replies and share an estimated response date. They will appreciate you notifying them rather than leaving them hanging indefinitely. Keep delays rare, but when unavoidable, communication preserves goodwill.

Follow Up on Open Matters

Keep track of pending inquiries or issues needing follow-up once the initial conversation concludes. Set reminders if needed. Reach out for a follow-up if you don't get a reply after a couple of days. Customers can simply forget sometimes.

Don't ignore your customers. Following through attentively strengthens relationships and satisfaction, even if complex issues take extended conversations to address.

Find a Sustainable Work-Life Balance

A major burnout risk for Etsy entrepreneurs is feeling tethered to constant communication. Balance timely replies with reasonable boundaries. Limit checking messages during designated family time or evenings. Let calls go to voicemail and respond the next day.

Make use of vacation mode when traveling or taking a break. Your customers will understand that you have a life and you need downtime. Just communicate delays transparently when you won't be as available.

Leverage Helpful Automation Tools

Using automation helps lighten the communication load so you can still reply efficiently when busy. Configure away messages for when you're unavailable. Set up pre-planned responses for common questions.

Enable shop notifications about sales and messages to keep on top of new inquiries. Use Etsy's template message feature when addressing similar issues. Look into third-party apps that can assist with customer communication. The right systems support consistency and sustainability.

Recover Well from Any Lapses

Despite your best efforts, you may occasionally miss a message or encounter unavoidable delays. How you recover matters. Apologize for the oversight and address their question or concern immediately. Reflect on how you can improve your system to prevent repeat issues.

Following up attentively typically resolves frustration. Everyone needs patience and grace sometimes. Help customers by caring about and focusing on their needs despite the hiccups.

Etsy customers value being able to easily communicate with the real small business owner behind a shop. By replying quickly, proactively setting expectations, following up thoughtfully, leveraging helpful tools, and sincerely recovering from lapses, you can provide timely communication without sacrificing your sanity.

Your customers will be grateful for your efforts to balance responsiveness and integrity as a one-person operation. With focus and care, great service doesn't have to mean being available 24/7.

CHAPTER 7

ADVANCED ETSY STRATEGIES

As your Etsy shop grows, implementing advanced tactics can take your business to the next level. This chapter reveals powerful strategies used by successful sellers to drive ongoing sales and stand out from competitors. You'll learn to track top competitors' listings and optimize against them using ERank and discover untapped profitable niches with tools like Everbee and Allura.

Create urgency with daily limited-time sales and promotions. Brainstorm truly unique products that entice buyers searching for something different. Strategically lower prices to increase reviews and conversion rates. With these advanced techniques, you can actively identify opportunities for improvement and growth not visible before.

Applying this knowledge will empower you to make strategic decisions that maximize visibility, drive quality traffic, boost conversion rates, and ultimately increase profitability month-over-month.

Tracking Your Competitors (ERank)

Opening an Etsy shop brings the exciting prospect of selling your handmade or vintage goods to a global audience. But with over 5 million active sellers on Etsy, you'll need to find ways to make your shop stand out. This is where researching your competitors becomes critical. By understanding what the other top shops in your niche are doing, you can make smart decisions to differentiate your shop and listings.

You need to learn how to use the powerful analytics tool ERank to comprehensively track and analyze your Etsy competitors. ERank provides invaluable intelligence to inform your product offerings, SEO optimization, promotion strategies, and branding.

Research Top Shops in Your Niche

Before starting, it's wise to scope out the competition and get a feel for your niche. Conduct Etsy searches for top sellers making products similar to yours. Take notes on factors like what items they offer, their price points, branding aesthetics, and key SEO elements like tag optimization and listing titles. Study their top-rated listings and product photography. This initial analysis will reveal what the leading Etsy shops in your category are doing right. You can then identify gaps where you may have an opportunity to differentiate.

Track Competitor Shop Metrics with ERank

Once your Etsy shop is up and running, you'll want to dig deeper into your competitors' performance over time. ERank has a "Competitors" feature that allows you to input up to 10 competitor Etsy shop names and track high-level metrics for each. To add shops, simply go to ERank's Competitors page, enter the shop names, and click "Add Competitors." You'll then have a dashboard displaying key data for each shop, including the total number of listings, sales, conversion rate, revenue, and average price point.

Check back regularly to see how your competitors' shops are growing and evolving. Are they increasing listings and sales month over month? How are their conversion rates changing? Monitoring the trends for top sellers in your niche provides benchmark data to use for your own shop's progress and growth strategies.

Compare Your Performance Against Competitors

One of the most useful aspects of tracking competitors in ERank is being able to compare their performance stats directly against your own. You can quickly view side-by-side metrics like your conversion rate versus your competitors' rates. If they are outperforming substantially in certain areas, you have an opportunity to optimize.

For example, if your competitor has 500 listings but your shop only has 50, you may need to increase production. Or, if their conversion rate is 6% versus your 2%, you likely have room to improve your SEO, photography, and listing quality. Let your competitors' successes show you how to boost your own shop's results.

Analyze Your Competitors' Popular Listings

Beyond high-level metrics, you can also leverage ERank to analyze the specifics of your competitors' most successful listings. Go to ERank's "Reverse Etsy Search" tool and input a competitor's shop name to pull up all of their listings. You can then sort their listings by "Most Favorited" or "Most Sales."

Take time to study the listings that resonate most with buyers. Look at how many tags they use, their keyword optimization tactics, what price points perform best, their photography style, and their listing titles and descriptions.

This research will provide a blueprint for what convinces shoppers to favorite and purchase items similar to yours. You may find opportunities to improve your SEO based on proven keywords your competitors are ranking for. You may even get product design inspiration from studying their best-sellers. Savvy Etsy sellers are always analyzing competitors' popular listings to inform their production plans, SEO approach, and listing strategies.

Monitor Your Competitors' New Listings

Another helpful report is ERank's "New Etsy Listings", which shows the latest listings from all shops in real time. You can filter by your competitor's shop name to see when they are launching new products. Monitoring this report allows you to quickly identify emerging trends and new product releases in your niche.

If a competitor starts listing trendy ceramic wall planters, you may want to consider developing a unique version yourself before the trend is saturated. If you notice a competitor increasing the output of pet products, you'll have an early signal that those items are growing in demand. Keep tabs on your rivals' new listings to stay ahead of the curve.

Track Competitors' Promotion Strategies

In addition to monitoring listings, you can track your Etsy competitors' promotion strategies using ERank's "Etsy Seller Promotions" tool. Many top Etsy shops run frequent sales, coupons, and promotions to boost visibility and drive purchases. Filter this report to see your competitors' current promotions including the discount percent, applicable product categories, and expiration dates.

This highlights when your competitors offer discounts and on what types of items. You may find certain competitors always run sales on slow-moving products at the end of each month to boost sales volume. Their timing and discount strategies can inform your promotion plans.

Research Their Social Media Presence

Your competitors' social media presence is another important area to keep an eye on. Use Instagram analytics tools to gauge competitors' follower counts and engagement rates. Check Facebook analytics as well for their fan growth and engagement.

Identify the Etsy sellers succeeding with social media in your niche – study what platforms they are active on, their posting cadence, their content formats, and their overall brand aesthetics.

Strong social followings signal buyer demand and industry authority. Comparing your social stats against competitors' highlights where you have room to expand your social presence and following.

Turn Competitor Insights into Shop Improvements

Conducting ongoing competitor research provides information to fuel your Etsy shop's growth and advancement. Use the insights gleaned from tools like ERank to continually refine your strategies around product selection, SEO optimization, conversion, promotions, and social media expansion.

The more you know about what your competitors are doing and what's working for them, the smarter you are about carving out your unique niche and positioning your shop for success.

Find Profitable Niches (Use Tools Like - Everbee, Allura)

When opening an Etsy shop, one of the most important decisions you'll make is identifying your niche and target market. With over 60 million active buyers searching across thousands of product categories, finding a profitable, less competitive niche is crucial to your shop's success.

Conduct Market Research on Etsy

Before settling on a specific niche, spend time researching current market trends on Etsy. Use the search bar to find top-selling items and best-selling independent shops across different product categories that interest you. Pay attention to the number of sales and reviews for popular listings, as this indicates market demand. Make notes on:

- Which categories have the most sales and traffic.

- The types of items selling well within broader categories.

- Pricing and buyer demand across niches.

- Current trends and product gaps you could fill.

This market research will reveal rising, high-potential niches versus saturated markets. It also helps you identify underserved niches where demand exists but competitive offerings are still relatively low.

Use Etsy Rank and ERank to Assess Categories

Etsy Rank and ERank are two invaluable tools for niche research. They allow you to analyze category data like the number of shops, search volume, listings, and favorited items.

For example, search for a broad category like "women's clothing" on Etsy Rank. It will show you metrics like:

- 1.2M+ active shops

- 21M+ monthly searches

- 534K+ items favorited in the past month

This massive volume indicates a lot of competition. Now search a narrower niche like "gothic dresses." The data shows:

- 82K active shops

- 364K monthly searches

- 15K+ recent favorites

The narrower niche has far less competition. Use Etsy Rank and ERank to compare metrics for multiple sub-niches and identify ones with healthy demand but lower competition.

Leverage Everbee for Niche Research

Everbee is a powerful niche research tool specifically designed for Etsy sellers. It lets you enter any keyword or product and instantly see key metrics like:

- Number of competing Etsy listings

- Estimated monthly Etsy searches

- Estimated monthly sales

- Top performing related keywords

This reveals untapped niche opportunities. For example, Everbee may show 400 competing listings and 600 monthly searches for "owl pillows." But the related keyword "owl throw pillow covers" has just 100 listings and 400 searches. This suggests an opportunity to focus specifically on covers.

Everbee also identifies related keywords and niche spin-off ideas you may not have considered. Use it early on to validate profitable, uncongested niches.

Apply the 'Micro Niche' Strategy

A proven Etsy strategy is targeting a very small, specialized niche or 'micro-niche' with highly targeted products. This allows you to carve out a niche that larger manufacturers can't compete with.

For example, instead of selling general jewelry, focus specifically on minimalist rings for pharmacists. Or provide planners for left-handed nuns. Tiny niches allow you to uniquely cater your products, marketing, and SEO to a clearly defined audience.

Research Competition on Social Media

Research beyond Etsy to assess niche demand and competitors on other sales platforms.

Search for hashtags related to your niche on Instagram to see engaged communities. Look for niche-specific groups on Facebook to get insights directly from your target buyers.

Check Google Trends data for search volume related to your niche over time. Study competitors selling niche products on their sites or other marketplaces.

Thorough cross-channel research gives you a complete view of your niche's potential.

Use Allura for Customer Insights

Allura is an excellent complementary tool for niche research. It offers an Etsy-integrated customer insights dashboard showing your shop's buyer demographics like age, gender, and location.

It also provides market research capabilities. You can enter any competitor domain name or keyword related to your niche. Allura will then estimate the demographics and interests of that competitor's target market.

These psychographic insights help you better understand potential niche buyers. You can then validate or refine your target customer profile based on the data.

Choose an Alignment Niche

Consider your interests, values, skills, and expertise when choosing a niche. Focused niches aligned with your passions have the highest likelihood of success.

For example, a seamstress with photography skills could open a shop for camera wrist straps featuring original printed fabric designs. This niche perfectly aligns her skills while catering to the photographer's target market she relates with.

Let your alignment guide you to a fulfilling, credible niche.

Assess Manufacturing Capabilities

Can you make quality products at a reasonable cost? Research factors like:

- Cost of required materials

- Production time per item

- Tools and space needed

- Shipping and packaging requirements

Consider outsourcing production if any aspects are prohibitively expensive or complex. But maintain control of design and quality where possible.

Choose a niche that fits your production capabilities while maximizing profits.

Estimate Market Size and Growth

Use market research data to estimate your niche's potential yearly sales. Everbee and Etsy Rank provide monthly search and sales estimates.

For example, a niche with 500 monthly searches at a $50 average order value would result in $30K in potential annual sales. Is the estimated yearly revenue enough to support your goals?

Also, look for rising niches indicating growth rather than stagnating or declining searches. Expanding niches offer longevity.

Evaluate Customer Lifetime Value

While transactional profit is crucial, also consider a niche's customer lifetime value. For example, pet owners or brides have repeat purchase potential over months or years.

Niches with high customer LTV allow you to cross-sell additional items over time or retain customers through new product releases.

Choose niches with both solid immediate sales potential and long-term loyalty.

Validate Your Niche Before Committing

Before investing significant time or money, validate your niche choice by:

- Listing test products and use Etsy or Google ads to gauge actual demand.

- Joining niche social groups to survey potential customers directly.

- Checking Google Trends data again for any decline in related searches.

- Analyzing competition and reviewing volume changes month-over-month.

Make sure that your niche choice remains financially viable and has low competition before fully committing.

Remain Flexible in an Evolving Market

No niche stays hot forever. Stay aware of market shifts by using the following tips:

- Monitor your niche metrics and competition.

- Notice when sales slow and review trends.

- Be ready to quickly expand or pivot your offerings.

- Consider expanding into complementary niche markets.

Being flexible allows you to adapt when your niche inevitably evolves.

Final Tips for Choosing Your Niche

- Research broadly at first, then narrow down.

- Use Etsy search data, Etsy Rank, and Everbee to assess niche viability.

- Identify rising niches before they become too saturated.

- Target specialized micro niches when possible.

- Choose an aligned niche that matches your interests and skills.

- Validate niche demand before fully diving in.

- Remain flexible and ready to adjust your focus over time.

Choosing the right profitable Etsy niche is crucial to your shop's success. With thorough research and the right tools, you can confidently identify a niche that aligns with your passions and has strong sales potential. Use these tips and resources to find your ideal niche, validate its viability, and start selling successfully.

Run Daily Sale Discount

As an Etsy seller, you know that running strategic promotions and sales is critical for boosting visibility and conversions in your shop. One effective tactic used by top Etsy sellers is offering daily discounts or limited-time deals. This creates a valuable sense of urgency and excitement for customers.

The Power of Urgency in E-commerce

In the world of online retail, shoppers have endless options at their fingertips. Attention spans are short, and distractions are everywhere. This makes it difficult for any single shop to capture focus.

That is why creating a sense of urgency and scarcity through limited-time offers is so powerful. Daily deals tap into our instinctual drive as consumers to snap up scarce products and avoid missing out.

When customers feel they need to act now or lose their chance, they are much more likely to purchase. Limited-time discounts drive conversion.

Offer a Deal of the Day

A simple yet effective tactic is having a Deal of the Day - one item or product collection available at a discounted price until midnight.

This deal format is popular because it's easy for customers to understand, and it capitalizes on fear of missing out. Make it clear the deal expires at the end of the day to encourage quick purchase decisions.

Offer your Deal of the Day on a specific product page or your shop homepage via a banner or badge, and promote it on social media. The time-limited nature makes it perfect for showcasing in emails and ads as well.

Rotate different items to continually create new urgency and interest.

Discount Slow Movers to Clear Inventory

Another smart way to leverage daily deals is discounting slow-moving inventory to spur sales.

Review your inventory reports and identify items that haven't sold well over the past month. Select a few stagnant products each day to offer as Daily Deals at 15-25% off.

Featuring slow movers as daily deals can boost their sales. This clears out inventory gathering dust.

Develop Themed Sales Events

Move beyond single product deals into themed daily sales focused around:

- Specific product types: "Hat Day Sale!"

- Holidays: "Valentine's Decor Up to 30% Off"

- Inventory groups: "All Clearance Items 50% Off Today Only"

Themed sales add more variety and give you the flexibility to discount broader segments of products each day.

Create an editorial calendar of upcoming themed daily events. Promote them on social media and your shop home page, and use eye-catching badges and banners that convey the discount and urgency.

Themed sales build anticipation and get customers checking back daily so they don't miss their favorite products.

Link Deals to Weekdays

Consider linking certain deals to specific weekdays that customers can come to expect and watch for:

- "Wallet Wednesday" - 15% off all small leather goods

- "Free Shipping Friday" on orders over $35

- "Seasonal Sundays" with deals on holiday décor

Consistent weekday sales drive habitual traffic as customers eagerly await their favorite deals.

Surprise Customers with Flash Sales

In addition to planned daily deals, sprinkle in some surprise sales to delight customers.

Send out flash deal announcements on social media and email for extra spontaneity. For example:

"Surprise 2-hour sale! Take 25% off all jewelry NOW through 5 pm EST!"

These spur-of-the-moment deals capitalize even more on excitement and urgency. Customers will be sure to follow you closely so they catch the next spontaneous sale.

Offer Site-Wide Sales

For major seasonal events or milestones, consider site-wide sales. For example:

- "Black Friday Sale - 20% Off Your Entire Order!"

- "Cyber Monday at MountainArtShop - Everything 30% Off!"

Site-wide sales create fanfare and get all of your products in front of customers at once. They also encourage larger-order values. Use them sparingly for occasions like holidays, birthdays, or anniversaries to preserve their novelty.

Promote Exclusively to Loyal Customers

Loyalty programs allow you to offer exclusive daily deals just for VIP members. You can also send members-only discount codes for single use.

This makes loyal customers feel valued with early access and personalized offers. It also incentivizes purchases with even greater urgency, knowing it's a deal others won't receive.

Let Urgency Drive Social Promos

All daily deals should be heavily promoted on social media. You can take it a step further by incorporating urgency into social giveaways.

For example, post:

"FLASH GIVEAWAY! We're giving away this $50 gift card TODAY ONLY. Like this post and tag 3 friends now - the winner announced in 1 hour!"

Social contests with very short entry windows and caps on the number of winners build excitement around sales and promotions.

Track Performance of Deals

Closely track the performance of all daily sales and identify your most effective deals.

For each limited-time sale or deal, record metrics like:

- Total promotional sales

- Number of items sold

- Conversion rate

- Average order value

Over time, you'll see which product types, discount levels, and promotion channels drive the highest conversions and revenue. Refine your daily deal strategy accordingly.

Create Unique Products that Stand Out

One of the most important elements in running a successful Etsy shop is offering unique products that captivate buyers and help you stand out from the competition. With over 60 million active shoppers now browsing Etsy, it takes creative and distinctive products to get noticed.

Research What Makes a Product Unique

Start by analyzing which qualities make a product truly unique and memorable in the eyes of shoppers. Some key elements that set items apart include:

1. **Distinctive Design Features**

   Special shapes, patterns, colors, or structural elements distinguish the item from mainstream offerings. An example is a necklace made with an unusual prong setting for the pendant.

2. **Rare Materials**

   Using exotic, heirloom, or reclaimed materials in uncommon ways, such as earrings fabricated from antique typewriter keys.

3. **Niche Appeal**

   Catering to a highly specific target customer, like planners designed just for reptile owners.

4. **Handmade Elements**

   Proof of handcrafting gives items a one-of-a-kind character. A good example is a custom wood-burned wedding sign with a couple's portrait etched by hand.

5. **Personalization**

   Any options for adding customizable details make each item singular, such as cake toppers printed with the couple's names and wedding dates.

6. **Limited Quantities**

Declaring pieces as limited edition, made-to-order, or produced in small batches, like a shirt run featuring only 10 printed copies.

It often comes down to very intentional design choices and production approaches aimed at creating truly memorable merchandise. Study what makes similar products in your niche feel mass-manufactured versus special. Then, build uniqueness into your manufacturing process.

Focus Being Different

Beyond just products, you want your entire Etsy shop brand to revolve around being fresh and different.

Brainstorm creative and memorable names. Choose visual branding like your logo, color palette, and font styling with an eye for the unconventional.

Craft your shop banner, logo, and item photos to convey the unique vibe you want to be associated with your business. Every brand touchpoint should reinforce what makes you different.

Offer What Competitors Don't Have

One of the simplest but most effective approaches for making unique products is tapping into gaps in your market niche not served by competitors.

Spend time researching current product offerings from other shops. Make notes on popular items that sellers in your space provide. Then, purposefully create products that deviate from what's widely available.

If owl pillow covers are saturating your market, design owl blanket ladders instead. If enamel pins are everywhere, try owl bag charms. You should be constantly looking for underserved needs or product gaps.

Give Existing Products a Unique Twist

Researching competitors can also reveal opportunities to put your spin on common products.

For example, basic ceramic planters are readily available. But what about hexagon-shaped planters in a glossy color gradient? Or geometric concrete planters with built-in irrigation systems?

Look for ways to take the expected and make it refreshingly unexpected. Identify current product trends and put your distinct twist on the concept.

Develop Signature Materials or Techniques

Consider developing unique custom materials or proprietary techniques for your products.

For example, make your signature recycled leather stamped with your logo or a new jewelry technique like wire woven chains.

Use these special materials and production methods across products to give your entire catalog a distinct character. Stylize product photos to play up your special touches.

Over time, your signature elements will become synonymous with your brand.

Specialize in Small Batches and Limited Editions

Producing products in small quantities inherently makes them more unique. This allows you to try small test batches of new ideas without over-committing.

Market your products as exclusive small-batch offerings, releasing just 10-50 units of each design. Serial number each piece and declare them as a limited run.

Scarcity triggers desire. Presenting products as rare, limited editions increases perceived value and demand.

Take Custom Orders

Offering made-to-order custom products is another excellent way to guarantee uniqueness.

Provide options for customers to request details like:

- Custom engravings

- Names or phrases

- Specified colors or fabrics

- Personalized fit or sizing

Made-to-order items have instant appeal as customers can create their perfect one-of-a-kind piece. Make sure to promote any custom offerings and showcase past bespoke orders.

Add Personal History to Products

Infusing items with backstories and history adds character. Imagine a refurbished antique dresser with photos of the restoration process or a description of its origins.

When you revive or repurpose materials, share their stories. For handmade goods, convey your inspiration and highlight artisanal touches.

These stories help customers connect with the products as special and meaningful. Their uniqueness becomes personal.

Go Vintage

Vintage and antique goods offer built-in uniqueness since they are inherently one-of-a-kind items. Curate forgotten treasures and give them new life.

Search estate sales, thrift stores, and auctions for unusual goods. Restore or upcycle them into modern pieces customers will appreciate.

Vintage appeals to the desire for items with character and historical charm. The right restoration can transform castoffs into highly distinctive offerings.

Collaborate with Other Artisans

Partner with fellow Etsy artisans to co-design products combining both your skills and styles. This fusion of perspectives is guaranteed to produce uniquely original work.

For example, collaborate with a leatherworker to create jewelry rolls featuring their leather craft and your embroidered designs.

Market products as exclusive collaborative. Share the artisan's shop to cross-promote. Limited collaborations intrigue customers eager for newness.

Curate Complementary Product Suites

Design products intentionally to complement each other for bundled sets or mini collections.

For example, create a baby nursery suite with swaddle blankets, sleep sacks, crib sheets, and wall art in matching prints. Or ceramic planter sets with coordinating pots, trays, and hangers.

Shops specializing in thoughtfully curated suites have a distinct edge. Customers love shopping for coordinated lifestyle looks.

Design Packaging for Impact

Unique packaging choices strengthen product distinction. Use unexpected materials like patterned tins or embroidered pouches. Include special touches like custom stickers, thank-you notes, or gifts with each order.

Spend just as much creativity on your packaging as on your products. Elevated packaging reflects the care you put into each order.

Promote Your Product Development Process

Content marketing that provides behind-the-scenes looks at your prototyping, manufacturing, and design process is highly effective.

Share in-progress photos on social media, videos of products being made, or Instagram Stories of new materials being sourced.

This gives customers insight into the care and craft behind each unique item. Let them follow the journey.

Analyze Customer Feedback

Product reviews, questions, and conversations with customers provide valuable insights into what shoppers find most appealing and unique about your items.

Regularly review feedback and customer comments to identify your products' most distinctive features. Take note of customization requests.

Let this input guide your efforts to refine offerings and highlight uniqueness even more.

Continuously Innovate and Improve

Strive to continually enhance products, introduce new design elements, and avoid stagnating.

Experiment with fresh materials, shapes, colors, and production methods. Always progress toward better uniqueness.

Make it expected that customers will find new surprises and innovations anytime they visit your shop.

Lower Price to Breakeven for Sales

Pricing is an art and science for Etsy sellers. You need prices high enough to operate profitably but not so high that they deter buyers. This next section will explore how to leverage break-even analysis to determine optimal pricing that balances profitability with generating the reviews and sales volume needed to boost your Etsy shop.

Understand Your Breakeven Point

The breakeven point is the unit price where your gross profit from each sale exactly covers your fixed and variable expenses. You don't make money at this price, but you don't lose any, either.

To determine your breakeven:

- Calculate your fixed costs like shop fees, software, and marketing.

- Determine your variable product costs, like materials and labor.

- Divide total fixed + variable costs by your sales volume target.

- This gives you the minimum break-even unit price. Any price above generates profit.

Set Your Initial Pricing Above Breakeven

You want to be profitable, so initially, price products above breakeven to earn income.

Factor in your desired profit margin, and add a premium for unique value. Get a sense of competitor pricing.

Price high enough to earn a fair profit while remaining competitive within your niche.

Offer Payment Plans to Increase Accessibility

Higher prices may deter some shoppers. Offer payment plans through Affirm or Klarna to improve accessibility.

This allows you to keep pricing intact while letting customers divide costs into installments. Broaden your audience by reducing the upfront burden.

Gradually Lower Prices to Drive Volume

Over time, consider gradually lowering prices closer to your breakeven point to boost order volume.

More unit sales at lower profit margins can potentially generate higher revenue overall. Increased transactions also benefit your Etsy search ranking.

And most importantly - more sales means more reviews.

Reviews Are Vital to Etsy Success

Product reviews are essential for Etsy shops to build credibility and SEO. They're evidence of satisfied customers, provide social proof, and boost search ranking.

Yet over 60% of Etsy shoppers say they won't purchase from shops with few or no reviews.

This is why driving sales volume through lower prices is a proven tactic to kick-start your critical initial reviews.

Make Sure Lower Prices Beat Competitors

When lowering prices for volume, make sure your prices beat competitors.

Research current competitor pricing using Etsy data tools. Price your products competitively, but always aim to undercut rivals.

Win on value by offering better prices than competitors while earning reviews. As credibility grows, you can gradually increase prices again.

Reduce Production Costs First

Before reducing prices, examine ways to lower production costs.

Can you source cheaper materials? Streamline processes? Order larger material quantities at volume discounts? Reduce packaging costs?

Lower expenses mean greater profit at any given price point. Maximize these efficiencies so you can minimize necessary price drops.

Maintain Perceived Value by Bundling

When lowering prices, use creative bundling to maintain an aura of higher value. Bundle items together, offering the suite at a full or slightly discounted price. This frames the items as worth more together than individually at lower costs.

Bundling also incentivizes higher order values and larger review-generating transactions.

Structure Smart Promotional Pricing

Promotional pricing done right can increase volume without denigrating brand value.

Avoid site-wide fire sales that can cheapen brand image. Instead, offer:

- Tiered discounts to incentivize higher orders

- First-time customer promos to spur testing

- Loyalty bonuses like annual % discounts or free products

Promote discounts privately via email or social media ads. Smart promotional pricing brings in sales while maintaining prestige.

Feature Lower-Priced Products Discreetly

Merchandise lower-priced products less prominently to avoid brand dilution.

Bury price-driving items on secondary pages or tabs. Feature prestigious full-price products most visibly across your shop and social channels.

This balanced approach gets the profits of high-ticket premium items while discreetly driving reviews via low-priced purchases.

Share Customer Stories and Reviews

To maximize the impact of growing reviews, actively feature and share positive customer stories.

Ask satisfied buyers for testimonials. Re-share great reviews on social media. Collect these in an "Our Customers" section on your shop.

Amplifying genuine customer stories helps convert social proof into sales. Let your raving fans showcase value.

Analyze Review Rates to Guide Pricing

Actively monitor how pricing changes impact review rates over time.

Lower prices should generate a steady uptick in conversion and reviews. If gains flatten, reassess pricing and discounts.

Consistently analyze review data to inform ongoing price adjustments. Reviews are the lifeline, so track pricing's impact.

Increase Prices Again Once Credibility Is Established

Once your shop has over 50+ solid 4-5 star reviews, begin gradually increasing prices again.

Your credibility is now established. You can likely retain customers at higher price points. Slowly reduce discounts over time.

Just make sure that pricing remains competitive and continues driving healthy order volumes even as you restore profitability.

CONCLUSION

Starting and growing a successful Etsy shop that can reach six-figure sales is a great opportunity for crafters, artists, and entrepreneurs. By leveraging Etsy's built-in audience of over 60 million active buyers, creative businesses can flourish selling handmade, vintage, or custom-designed goods in a global marketplace. However, building a profitable Etsy shop takes knowledge, preparation, and employing the right strategies at each stage.

In this comprehensive guide, you go through the entire process of establishing and expanding an Etsy business. The foundation begins with conducting crucial upfront research to identify winning, in-demand products and target buyer demographics within Etsy's market. This informs branding, shop design, product development, and positioning. Once a brand vision is in place, securing reliable production partners and suppliers provides the capacity to scale.

With the backend established, the next focus is meticulously building out your Etsy shop, fine-tuning listings for maximum visibility, and cultivating a polished brand aesthetic that resonates. Conveying your unique story and value proposition attracts your ideal audience. With products listed and brand polished, driving those critical first sales requires smart marketing across ads, social promotion, and leveraging reviews for social proof.

As order volume grows, properly managing operations and customer service becomes paramount. This guide includes tips for smooth day-to-day management, from fulfillment to communications to handling issues like negative reviews or copyright claims professionally.

Running your Etsy venture like an optimized business is what enables explosive growth.

For sellers aiming for massive scale, advanced strategies help differentiate exceptional Etsy shops. Competitor analysis, niche evaluation, continually creating distinctive products, strategic pricing tactics, and innovation are all principles used by today's highest-revenue sellers. Combining entrepreneurial creativity with analytical business rigor is at the core of unlocking six and seven-figure success.

While this guide covers a proven framework, your unique vision and execution will ultimately determine your shop's success. With diligence and passion, you can make significant earnings. Lean into your creativity, leverage the resources and knowledge presented here, and deliver incredible value to buyers through your unique offerings.

By combining strategic foundations with your flair and effort, your Etsy business can flourish and reach impressive heights. Consider this your roadmap - now let your originality and dedication pave the way to remarkable achievements.

Made in the USA
Columbia, SC
22 October 2024

44882046R00089